Natalie is a master of reinvention, and this book is her masterpiece. Anyone who wants more freedom should read it!

— **Chris Guillebeau, Author of *Side Hustle* and *The $100 Startup***

Simply put, Natalie Sisson helps entrepreneurs live the life they've imagined. Packed with wisdom and useful systems to free up your time and help you focus on your passions, The Freedom Plan is a powerful way forward.

— **Dorie Clark, Adjunct Professor at Duke University's Fuqua School of Business and Author, *Entrepreneurial You* and *Reinventing You***

Freedom is my number one value, so of course, I jumped on Natalie's book! Natalie is such a leader in helping us find ease and abundance in our businesses without the old-skool burn out that so many entrepreneurs face. Here's to less work and more money!

— **Denise Duffield-Thomas, Author *Chillpreneur* and *Get Rich, Lucky Bitch***

Natalie is setting the world ON FIRE one freedom lover at a time. I've been able to find freedom by building a team to support my efforts and spread my message to the world. In The Freedom Plan, Natalie breaks down how to find, hire and build YOUR Global Dream Team, like I've built mine. If you love freedom, you'll LOVE this book!

— **John Lee Dumas, Entrepreneurs on Fire | EOFire.com**

There's nobody I've learned more from about how to lead a freedom-based business (and life) than Natalie Sisson. Through her mix of expert advice, fascinating research, personal and client success stories, freedom-infused activities, and robust resources, in Natalie's The Freedom Plan you'll develop your own vision for freedom and learn practical and effective ways to align (and monetize!) work you love with the life you want (and are entitled!) to lead.

— **Alexia Vernon, Speaker and Author of** *Step into Your Moxie* **at AlexiaVernon.com**

If you are unhappy with the 'conventional' way of earning and income, The Freedom Plan offers a modern and practical pathway to do things differently. From mindset changes through to becoming an expert then earning money from your business, Natalie has you covered.

— **James Schramko, Founder of SuperFastBusiness and Author of bestseller:** *Work Less, Make More.*

If you feel you want more freedom in how you work but aren't sure how to make that happen from where you are now - read this book. It's a rare book that combines smart business thinking while also placing the biggest asset in your business (aka you) at the centre of it all.

— **Marianne Cantwell, Author of** *Be a Free Range Human.*

Natalie Sisson not only KNOWS all about freedom (I always look at her slightly green with envy) but she also knows how to teach YOU about it. For Natalie, the word "impossible" isn't in her vocabulary. If you want a structured plan to live a life on your terms, then this is it.

— **Matthew Kimberley, Author of** *How to Get A Grip,* **Coach, Speaker at MatthewKimberley.com**

Natalie's eye-opening book reveals how anyone can achieve greater levels of financial and time freedom in their business.

— Selena Soo, Creator of Impacting Millions

"The Freedom Plan is a comprehensive guide for any business owner who wants liberation from daily demands and more freedom. Natalie helps you create the right vision, systems, and team for you and your business, and she shares what works and what to watch out for. Each chapter walks you through practical steps to your version of freedom, and through Natalie's experience you'll find the shortcut to your own happiness. I highly recommend this book to anyone who feels stuck and wants to scale without burning out or giving up their freedom."

— Nathalie Lussier, Founder AccessAlly.com

There are two people that come to my mind as the ultimate freedom entrepreneur - Richard Branson and Natalie Sisson. Before I had the courage to start my own business Natalie inspired me with her blog to believe that building a freedom business is possible for anyone. In her book The Freedom Plan, she lays out the exact steps on how to scale your business to the point where you can actually enjoy the freedom of being a business owner and live your dream life.

— Sigrun Gudjonsdottir, Business Strategist, Mastermind Coach, TEDx Speaker

"I've know Natalie for several years and have always admired how fully she lives her freedom lifestyle. This book is your chance to learn from someone who has walked the walk. Natalie gives you all the steps, tools, and mindset shifts you need to make your freedom lifestyle a reality starting today. Don't wait until 'someday later' to finally enjoy your ideal flavor of freedom. Read this book and put it into action today."

— Jason Van Orden, Business Strategist to Thought Leaders

Starting a business that gives you the freedom to work from anywhere in the world (even home) is about more than just travel. You also have the opportunity to take control of the most valuable asset of all...your time. That means more spent with loved ones and doing work that is meaningful to you. On top of that, unlike traditional jobs, your income potential has no limit. One BIG problem though...starting any type of business is NOT easy! But it is 100% possible with the right guidance. This book is your opportunity to learn from someone who has done it AND has helped thousands of others combine their ideal lifestyle with their work. If you're ready to get serious about making the "work from anywhere" lifestyle happen for yourself, here's your chance.

— **Jason Moore, zerototravel.com and Cofounder of Location Indie**

As one of the O.G. digital nomads in my space, Natalie ditches the fluff and gets straight to the point in Freedom Plan. It's literally a manual for creating not just a business but a freeing LIFESTYLE that I wish I had when I started my own online business years ago. If you're looking for the big-picture view of how to have it all, read this book.

— **Elise Darma, Online Business Educator at EliseDarma.com**

The concrete ideas and exercises in this book will give you the specific ACTIONS to take to begin building more freedom in your life. Natalie — and her impressive case studies in the book — will inspire you to step back and take a serious look at what you really want your life to be.

— **Nick Loper, Founder of SideHustleNation.com**

I am LOVING this book! I started using some of the questions to spark a discussion with my husband. It was eye opening to see 1) how just a few immediate tweaks will get me so close to my ideal day 2) where I have been dragging my feet and how fear has gotten in the way of experiencing deeper freedom right now. A few chapters in, I had revamped and reprioritized my schedule, and committed to finally hiring the next level of support I need in my business. The world needs this book. If you want more freedom, fulfillment, and success, read it, study it, make lots of notes and then actually do it. The information in its pages is invaluable and is worth thousands. Much more when you actually implement it.

— **Mandi Ellefson, Scalable Service Growth Strategist**

In all the years I've followed Natalie's work, it's clear that there are very few people in the world that understand the ins and outs of a lifestyle business better than her. This book is proof of that. Rather than just providing more inspiration, as so many authors do, she helps with the tactical strategy to get you where you want to go.

— **Sean Ogle, Founder of LocationRebel.com**

THE FREEDOM

PLAN

REDESIGN YOUR BUSINESS TO WORK LESS, EARN MORE AND BE FREE

NATALIE SISSON

Published by Motivational Press, Inc.
1777 Aurora Road
Melbourne, Florida, 32935
www.MotivationalPress.com

ISBN: 978-1-62865-576-6

CONTENTS

In loving memory of my father Peter, who

lived life to the fullest and

always stopped to smell the roses.

FOREWORD

Most people live the life they think they 'have to' live.

That old story we tell ourselves — that we need to work hard, put in the long hours, and hustle like crazy in order to be successful and happy — is dead.

We need a new story that starts with who and where we are now and expresses our vision for the future.

A story that defines what our ideal life looks like, and how we can achieve it through redesigning our business to fully support it.

We need a mindset shift that says WE are responsible for our own freedom, and that it is up to us to change how we live, act, work and be.

If you're like the thousands of entrepreneurs I've met, your business now is likely completely different from the business you started in the first place.

You wanted to make a dent in the world, to make an impact, to help others, leave a legacy and have more freedom.

But, somewhere along the way, your business hasn't given you the lifestyle you deserve, and now you likely:

- Feel trapped in a business that is essentially a job.

- Are stressed out, overwhelmed and always 'busy', but never making real progress.

- Love what you're doing, but work so hard that you don't have time for your friends, family or to even enjoy life.

- Have lost your mojo and purpose — why you started your business in the first place.

- Are stuck in the "trading time for dollars," business model.

If that sounds like you then it's time to create your unique Freedom Plan so you can live a fantastic life, while running a rewarding and profitable business.

That's what this Freedom Plan book is all about.

I promise you, that there will be a big difference between the current you and the future you, after you've read this book and created your own Freedom Plan.

You will:

- Believe YOU can live your dream lifestyle and run a successful business at the same time.

- Know exactly how and what you need to create your own unique freedom plan that gives you purpose and profit — all while living your perfect day, every day.

- Learn how to apply your skills, experience, and knowledge in the digital economy, and create a profitable freedom business based around YOU.

- Transition from relying on your business or "job," to a life of freedom, self-reliance, and total control.

- Create financial freedom and abundance, while doing good in the world, not only for yourself, but for those around you and your community.

Life is about enjoying rich experiences and adventures — right now, not tomorrow.

This book will walk you step-by-step through *designing your perfect lifestyle FIRST*, and then how to redesign your business to support you, while having fun and being rewarded financially.

It's all about defining and structuring your business around the vision you articulate for yourself, now and in the future. Whether you want to work full-time or build a business that makes money without you, so you can spend your time doing more of the things you love, with the people you enjoy — it's totally up to you.

The Freedom Plan book is designed to enlighten and inspire you to believe you can live in the present moment and create more freedom to truly live your ideal life.

It may even make you want to fire yourself as the boss of your own business and live a truly rewarding lifestyle where you work less, earn more and be free.

Better yet, it may help you realize how you could encourage and inspire others to live with more freedom and assist them in living life they desire.

It's time to make a change. Let's rewrite the conventional story. **Let's create our own freedom plan, on our own terms.**

COMPANION VIDEO SERIES

As you'll learn throughout this book, I'm a huge fan of taking action. Not later, but right now, while you're motivated, learning and even inspired.

There is no better time than now to create your own Freedom Plan, and while this book is packed with value, tactics, tips and examples, there is so much more I want to share with you.

So I've created a free video series to bring this book to life.

It contains templates, resources, and four practical video lessons to ensure you take what you learn and put into action today!

I promise it will not overwhelm you, but empower you to create your own Freedom Plan.

At any point you can head to thefreedomplan.co/start to sign up for free and get started.

STAGE 1

FREEDOM MINDSET

1

THE FREEDOM MINDSET TO MAKE YOUR DREAM LIFE A REALITY

Close your eyes and imagine you've just won a $20 million dollar lottery and the world is your oyster.

- Where in the world would you wake up?

- What would you spend your time doing?

- Who would you spend it with?

- What would it look like, smell like, sound like and feel like?

Over the past six years, I have asked hundreds of people this exact question. And guess what?

99% of them have no idea how to answer it. They have never thought about what their perfect day looks like in vivid detail, let alone their perfect life.

Why is that?

Because somewhere along the way, we stop chasing our dreams. We stop imagining what our perfect day looks like and we start handing over the reins to society, which told us what to do and how to live.

I have found myself in this place several times in my life, where I've given away my freedom.

So what exactly is freedom, you may ask.

According to the Oxford Dictionary:

> freedom
>
> ˈfriːdəm/
>
> noun
>
> > 1. the power or right to act, speak, or think as one wants.

These days, I'm obsessed with Freedom and its definition.

I spent close to seven years living out of my suitcase, with no fixed home, traveling to seventy countries around the world, all by myself.

I've experimented with living and working from anywhere and everywhere, all while designing and creating my perfect freedom business that supports my ideal lifestyle.

In early 2017, I decided to switch up my lifestyle completely and explore a new version of freedom.

I met my loving partner, after many years of enjoying single life, and together we took a big leap and bought a beautiful lifestyle property (a big house on 2.5 acres of land).

We then set about creating a beautiful lifestyle of freedom there, with dogs, chickens and growing our own fruit and vegetables.

We also planted roots and became part of the local entrepreneurial community, investing our time and energy into sustainable living, hosting retreats and creating a coworking space in our barn!

I started new business ventures collaboratively with others, which I can run from home, or anywhere I choose. I value this flexibility and freedom of choice very highly.

Both lifestyles have their benefits, and of course, their drawbacks. I feel privileged to have experienced them both.

Right now, living on this property (and others I own around the world) is my version of happiness, but it might not have been, had I not traveled the world like a vagabond for so many years.

As a result of the nomadic life I led, I now fully appreciate having a base, feeling grounded and at one with nature.

At the end of the day, what I know to be true is this:

I believe freedom is a right, not a privilege and it's up to YOU to create your own freedom plan, on your own terms.

The thing is, freedom is actually a state of mind. It has taken me many years to understand and experience that for myself.

To demonstrate this more fully, I want to share an excerpt from my TEDx talk, *The Surprising Truth About Freedom*, I did at Royal Tunbridge Wells in June 2016.

In many ways, it's the perfect premise for this book and all the gems you'll find in it.

It's also a very personal story about my journey from the corporate world, to the entrepreneurial one, and how I came to call myself a 'Freedomist.' I hope it'll resonate with you, and that you'll find your own lessons within.

Stage 1: Free Your Mind From The Conventional Ways Of Living

It's July 2008, I am in London at my dream job.

I have what so many people would say is "the good life." I have worked my way up the corporate ladder ending up in a high-paying, senior management position with lots of responsibility and a whole team under me...

But I am not happy.

The work isn't fulfilling anymore.

Something inside of me is dying.

I am actually losing my freedom.

Someone else is telling me when to wake up in the morning.

What to do

How to act

What to say

How to FEEL

Someone else dictates how much money I make and when I can go on holiday.

People show up like robots to work, check in and check out and weren't even present.

They are missing the most important moments of their own lives; we all are.

I am on the London tube on my typical commute to work, squished in like a sardine, in complete silence, avoiding all eye contact and then, it hits me.

I am wasting 45 minutes of my life, twice a day just on getting to and from work. That's 15.6 days in a year of my life entirely dedicated to being a sardine.

Even worse is the realization of how totally inefficient this "rat race" is.

Shops, post offices, banks, and dentists open up when I go to work and close almost right after I leave.

Which means, the only time to do anything is over lunchtime or straight after work when hordes of other people are doing the same thing.

People have been trapped in this traditional way of doing things for too long.

This is a race no-one is going to win.

I ask myself, "How did I get to this place?"

How did I lose my everyday freedom chasing after a job I thought I wanted, to earn money to buy things I didn't need and spend my time working for someone else, on their terms, and make zero impact on the world?

Have You Ever Felt Like This?

You're not alone. In Gallup's 2013 *State of the Global Workplace* study of 120,000 people from 142 countries, a staggering 48% of employees were unhappy in their jobs.

So what can you do if this is you?

The way I see it, you have two choices.

Choice #1: Quit. Escape Now!

OR

Choice #2: Make the most of what you have

- Ask for flexible working hours (so you can avoid the commute).

- Or work from home a few days a week.

- Find out if there's a way you can engage in more meaningful work that you enjoy.

So which option did I take?

I did what any other sane person who was unhappy at work would have done, even though I'd just been given a raise and bought a house in London.

I handed in my notice.

I sold everything I owned. Packed a suitcase, and took a one-way flight to Canada to play World Championship Ultimate Frisbee and live the dream.

Stage 2: Do Work You Love To Support Your Ideal Lifestyle

It's August 2008, and I've finally broken free from eight years in the corporate world, only to realize one very important thing — I am now homeless, unemployed, and have no freaking idea what I am going to do!

Thankfully, I met my business partner at a networking event, and we started a technology company called ConnectionPoint Systems and go on to build a Facebook app called FundRazr.

The next 18 months are a wild roller coaster ride in the world of a startup.

I love the fast pace.

I love the challenge.

I'm putting in every ounce of my experience and knowledge, but the problem is I'm working longer and longer hours, drinking too much bad coffee and playing less Ultimate Frisbee.

I soon realize that I have built myself another job. Only this time, I have 10X more the responsibility and far less freedom than in the 9-to-5.

My business partner notices the one thing I am truly passionate about, my blog. He suggests that I should go off and turn it into a business. And I say, "Great idea!"

We part ways amicably and off I go...with just a blog and no way of getting paid.

For the next six months, I go into full-time hustle mode, and right around the time my savings have dwindled down to just $17 dollars in my bank account, I secure my first consulting gig.

Then I run three completely sold-out business workshops, and suddenly, things are looking up.

I know this is the time I have to take a risk to get what I want.

I want to be location independent and have the freedom to work my business, but still make money, from anywhere in the world.

Once again, I pack a few possessions in a small suitcase and head off to Buenos Aires in Argentina to dance the tango, learn Spanish and eat a ton of empanadas.

At first, it feels totally exhilarating.

But in the end, I'm creating LESS freedom for myself.

The business has become the dictator of my life. I'm feeling trapped. I'm working too many hours and not earning enough money to justify going out.

And it doesn't get any better when I start traveling to other countries, staying weeks or months at a time.

There's this constant pull, between being a tourist versus an entrepreneur, and I feel guilty whenever I am doing too much of either.

Then, there's this moment of grace, where it hits me all at once and I realize…"this isn't freedom."

I'm working harder than ever, all by myself, and although I love it, something has to change or I'm going to burn out and start hating what I'm doing.

I knew at that moment that I was going to have to fight for my freedom.

I finally bit the bullet and hired my first contractor, my Virtual Assistant, Margaret.

In just 2 weeks, I taught her everything she needed to know to take over enough of my business so it wouldn't fall apart while I was gone.

And then, I put it all to the test.

I decided, in a moment of sheer craziness, to sign up for Tour d'Afrique, and cycled from Nairobi, Kenya to Cape Town, South Africa. A trip of 6,500km (4,000 miles) over two months.

It was a complete success.

At the end of the Tour, I had sexy tan lines, a massively sore butt, and so many flat tires that those riding with me named me Flatalie.

I got to ride past herds of wild elephants, packs of hyenas and even had a giraffe visit our camp one night.

Meanwhile I realised no-one missed my updates on social media, nobody cared that I hadn't tweeted or posted on Facebook and people didn't get upset that I hadn't emailed them back.

In fact, I had been making money online, while cycling 160 km plus every day, down Africa, on a personal challenge, and raising $12,000 for Women Win Charity.

I had never felt so free in my life as I did while cycling. And I'm super thankful for that experience because it taught me the power of having a business that allowed me freedom.

- I put systems in place.

- I created a virtual team.

- I built a sales funnel that worked on autopilot.

I worked myself out of a job and into the position of leading my company that educates others on how to create freedom in business and open doors for more adventure in life.

I've created a new version of freedom. An adjective, in fact — FREEDOMIST!

- I can live and work anywhere in the world.

- I make more money than I ever have.

- I have more free time, more fun and more adventure.

- I'm living the dream.

I can choose yoga in the morning, beaches at sunset and everything in between.

I get to hang out with amazing like-minded people, like the Denning family, from the US, who travel with their seven kids, while running their freelance business.

Sam and Janine, who work a few days a week from home and spend quality time with their kids.

Full-time professional house-sitters, Nat and Jodie, living for free around the world in incredible destinations, hanging out with adorable cats and dogs.

Paul and Sheryl, sailing around the world, making and selling TV shows from their yacht.

Designers, developers, and entrepreneurs, who travel the world, while building cool projects, like the Hacker Paradise community.

Which leads me into the next stage, and an entirely new take on freedom.

Stage 3: Design Your Own Version Of Freedom And Live It

It's summer of 2015, and I find myself in Portugal.

I've rented an apartment with amazing views over the city of Lisbon. I'm drinking sangria like it's going out of fashion.

I'm surrounded by good looking men, racing around on my scooter, hanging out at beautiful beaches and running my business from cafes and rooftop bars.

I think I've finally found a country I can live in, after close to six years of being homeless that feels like a second home to me, after New Zealand. It has all the elements I've missed or desired on my travels and I'm drawn to its energy.

This is a big deal for the Suitcase Entrepreneur, as I've built my brand around traveling the world.

But the fact is, I feel free. I'm happy.

A few weeks later, while speaking at a conference full of 500 digital nomads, just like me, I get the worst call of my life. It's from my family back home. My Dad has fallen ill.

My sister tells me he's in the hospital and they fear he doesn't have long to live.

Now, when you're literally on the other side of the world, far far away from the people you love most in your life, it's quite possibly the hardest thing in the world to deal with.

I felt like I shut down for three days, while I waited for news on whether I should jump on the first flight home.

I couldn't eat, I couldn't sleep, and could barely function.

Two days later, Mum rang from the hospital, crying, and asked me if I could come home.

I packed my things into my suitcase, dropped off my scooter, and left for New Zealand the following morning.

It was the longest thirty six hour journey of my life, and when I got home, I went straight to visit Dad.

Mum prepared me for the worse, letting me know that he may not be able to recognize me.

I was thankful he did.

The next five months were a different kind of rollercoaster, an emotional one. The doctor's couldn't officially tell us what was wrong with Dad, and he had three bouts of delerium.

On his third visit to the hospital, he never came out. That day, not only did I lose an incredible dad to cancer, but also one of my best friends, who I adored.

In the moments after Dad passed away, I had two very important life realizations.

#1 My definition of freedom had found new meaning.

Before, it was simply to do what I wanted, when I wanted, with who I wanted.

Now, it was the ability to drop everything and take time off my business to focus on family.

With my freedom business that I'd set up to support my lifestyle, I was able to do exactly what I wanted at that moment.

Had I still been in a job or in my first business, I realised I may not have been able to take more than two weeks off at such short notice, or even afford to jump on an expensive plane trip.

Which led me to the second realization.

#2. Your version of freedom is totally unique to you.

- For some people, it's sailing around the world.

- For others, it's living in a yurt in the forest.

- For some, it's the right to vote.

- To get married, or stay single.

- To have a beautiful home.

- To have no home at all.

- Or become the fastest changer of flat tires in the whole wide world.

It all comes down to how much you want to create your own freedom plan and make it a reality today...not tomorrow.

Ask yourself this, what would you do if you had an extra 10 hours a week and more income?

Imagine how your life would be?

How would you spend your day?

Who you would spend it with?

Where would you be?

How would you feel?

If your definition of freedom is not meeting your reality, I invite you to apply these 3 stages to your life.

1. Stage 1: Free your mind from the conventional ways of living.

2. Stage 2: Do work you love that supports your ideal lifestyle.

3. Stage 3: Define your own version of freedom and live it.

No more excuses.

No more "some day."

You do have time.

You do have a choice.

You do have the right to choose freedom.

2

DESIGNING YOUR OWN FREEDOM PLAN

Now that you've read my story, I'd like to know yours.

More importantly, if you could write your new story, what would it be?

This book is going to help you do that. If you're prepared to put in the effort and do the work, you too can create your ideal Freedom Plan.

I've written this book to help you get unstuck from your freelance career or business that's not meeting your needs and has you trading time for money.

If what you've built is nothing like you dreamed it was going to be, and instead it's become a never-ending slog that's sucking your energy and leaving you with little, to no free time to live your ideal lifestyle, then good news.

You're not alone.

Did you know that entrepreneurs are working an average of fifty-two hours a week? That's **63% longer than employees**, according to research by call handling firm Penelope.

I mean, that's ridiculous.

I'm pretty sure those of you in here, who have your own business, or do freelance work, aren't going to say on your deathbed, "Man, I wish I'd checked my email more!"

Your business should be designed to support your lifestyle goals, not take over your life!

The number one mistake people make when they design their dream business is to forget about aligning it to their *values, personality,* and *lifestyle desires*.

People either build a business or career that takes over their life OR they build a business that actually isn't suited to their entrepreneurial strengths.

As a result, it feels out of alignment with who they are and doesn't give them purpose.

I've met plenty of people making a lot of money from their business who are not happy.

And I don't want that for you.

What I want for you, is your business and pleasure to mix together like a delicious cocktail that leaves you feeling giddy.

And it all comes down to having the right mindset. The mindset of freedom. Let me introduce you to my, not so secret, formula for this.

The Sisson SMILE Formula

Directions: Apply liberally to your freedom-based lifestyle business, to relieve any pain or overwhelming feelings you might currently be experiencing.

S stands for your Sweet Spot.

The sweet spot is the intersection between what you enjoy doing, what you're good at or even great at, what people will pay you for, and what gives you a sense of purpose.

When you figure out your sweet spot, it illuminates what you should be doing and provides you with meaning, which gives you direction and focus.

As I said, you don't want to be in some soul-destroying business that really isn't lighting your fire.

M is for Meaningful.

There's got to be meaning behind it, whether it's meaningful for you, your clients and customers, or a greater purpose in the world.

When something is meaningful, it will make it much more valuable and easy for you to get in a state of flow, and commit to it daily.

In Chapter 4, I cover this in more depth, with real examples of people from a variety of backgrounds doing this right now.

I is for Impact.

Let's face it. We all want to make an impact on this world.

I want to make an impact in your life through this book and through the work I do.

You will make an impact in the lives of your friends, family, and children.

But for some of us, we want to do even more than that. We want to impact thousands or hundreds of thousands or even millions of people.

- Maybe you want to make an impact in the political world.

- Maybe you want to make an impact in the nonprofit world.

- Maybe you want to make an impact on society.

- Maybe you want to make an impact on the environment.

There are so many areas for you to put a dent in. I want you to think of how you are going to make an impact in this world. That is going to be the driving force behind what you do while reading this book and beyond.

L stands for Lifestyle

Even if your business or idea is hitting your sweet spot, is meaningful and going to make an impact, you still have to make sure it fits within your lifestyle.

You don't want to be doing this 24/7. Even when you truly love it. Or, trust me, you will burn out.

You want a business that supports the way you want to live and allows you to have the freedom to spend quality time with the people you love.

You want a freedom business that lets you work on other meaningful projects or initiatives that you want to be part of.

E is for Evolving.

I can guarantee as you devour this book, you are going to evolve. Your mindset will grow and expand. Your business or career is going to evolve.

What you want for your life, your future, and your goals, are going to evolve. And so, the business that you are going to build, needs to evolve with you.

So I want you to keep the SMILE Formula in mind as we develop your Freedom Plan together.

When you're struggling, when you're challenged, when you feel like giving up or when you're actually taking two steps backward, instead of one step forward, come back to this chapter and reaffirm why you're doing what you're doing.

What Qualities Do You Need To Be A Freedomist?

I started calling myself a Freedomist around three years ago, and in my mind the definition is this: *An individual who strives for freedom in their daily life and stays true to their purpose in all they do'.*

Throughout this book, I really want you to stay in touch with the key internal qualities you need to be truly free and continue to work on developing them.

These qualities do not appear overnight.

I have flexed these muscles. I have learned these skills. I have adopted these qualities into my life. Some of them I had inherently; others I've worked hard to build upon.

I am going to share with you the top qualities you need to be a Freedomist. There may be more, but honestly, I think it always comes back to these. So listen up.

☐ 1. A vision for your business and life, which you are willing to fight for.

Every time I see my mission, to help you reach your full potential through uncovering life-changing habits, routines and hacks to give you more daily freedom, I'm inspired.

I know I have work to do. I know I have an impact to make, and I need to get out there and spread my message far and wide.

The inspiration is really handy on the days when I just want to shrink away, and go and read a book in a corner, because I know my mission is way more important than that.

People are going to challenge you on this.

- They're going to challenge you on the way you're living your life.

- They're going to challenge you on what your business stands for.

- They're going to challenge you on the way you want to spend your time.

You are going to need to fight for it, and you need to know the reasons why you're doing it. You need a strong sense of purpose.

This holds true during those times when you are feeling doubt, fear or thinking about changing your mind. Simply come back to your purpose.

Why you're doing what you're doing?

Why is this important to you?

What do you envision for your life?

How are your current actions going to get you there?

☐ **2. Determination, persistence, and the willingness to hustle.**

Strategic hustling, as I call it, is a great quality to develop.

It doesn't have a bad connotation to it, and it's something that every single entrepreneur, I know, regularly applies to their business, maybe even beyond that, because when you're hustling, you're making things happen.

☐ **3. Courage to live your dream no matter what other people think.**

Other people will always have an opinion and they will share it with you, whether you asked them to or not. Even if they have no experience in the matter at hand.

I've been incredibly fortunate. Almost all my family and friends are supportive of my business, even if they don't always know exactly what it is I do.

But lo and behold, there's always somebody who will criticize, challenge or impose their fears on you in a negative way. They will try to detract you from what you're doing because they don't understand, they're jealous, or they want you to fail.

That's their problem, not yours. Give them the opportunity to change their mind, by educating them on what you do and why it's important.

You can even share what opportunities lie ahead of them, if they're willing to open their mind.

If they still don't understand, then simply thank them for their concern, then tell them that all you require is their support in the decision you've made to be a Freedomist.

If they can't, then remove them from your life. If that sounds too harsh or is not possible, restrict their impact on your life as much as possible.

They will not serve you, and they will do their best to pull you off track and derail you from your dreams. Don't give them that power!

Let me tell you, no one who changed the world, did so by listening to naysayers, critics or people who thought they knew better, but had never actually done anything important in their own lives... ever.

☐ 4. The ability to spend time by yourself and enjoy your own company.

This is a great quality to have. Not only as an entrepreneur, which can be a lonely road, even though it doesn't have to be, but also if you're going to travel, live in different countries, and create your new life in a place away from home.

It's really handy to be able to depend upon, enjoy your own company, and be more than OK spending time by yourself.

☐ 5. An independent nature and the strength of character to deal with daily challenges.

This one goes without saying. If you can't look after yourself and prioritize YOU first, then you certainly can't help anyone else.

If you're going to travel the world or be location independent, this becomes even more important, especially when you no longer have a daily routine and are forced into making multiple decisions in a day.

This habit improves with time and will benefit you personally and your business.

☐ 6. A keen desire to explore and experience new places or things.

Here, I'm referring to a sense of adventure in your daily life. Whether you plan to run your business, while traveling the world, or you prefer to work from home, I suggest you think like a global citizen and do new things regularly.

Even if you consider yourself a homebody and love your creature comforts, I recommend you become a 'local tourist' by getting out and about to discover new cafes, the theater, festivals or fun and entertaining events.

Join a local community group, go on a hike, anything to explore your area and get you out of your comfort zone.

There are so many rich experiences that come from getting out of your own bubble, meeting new people, going to new places and experiencing new cultures.

Obviously, the more curious you are, the more you're going to enjoy those experiences and be open to different cultures, sights, sounds, religions, food, weather, etc.

And you know what?

I actually think this is one of the key qualities that helps you as an entrepreneur.

The more open-minded you can be, and the more aware of things that aren't in your immediate business sphere, the more depth you can add to your work, your clients, and your imagination.

☐ **7. Strong decision-making, planning capabilities, and discipline that you can act on.**

This is going to be critical to your success. If you can continue to hone these skills, life will be more fantastic.

Traveling allows you to do this all the time as you have to make instant decisions on:

- Where you're going to stay.

- Which bus you're going to catch.

- What train you're going to jump on.

- Where you're going to spend the night.

- What activity you're going to do.

- How much you're going to pay for something.

Being in business is going to demand this from you when you're:

- Negotiating with suppliers or service providers.

- Deciding on which revenue streams to introduce or drop.

- Making decisions on who you're hiring.

- Deciding where your office is going to be based or if you won't have one.

- Figuring out what to focus on next, or which priorities you're going to tackle.

The better you can get at making informed decisions and quickly, the more rewarding your experience will be. It comes down to knowing your non-negotiables, and of course, having a Freedom Plan that you live by.

Along with this, is the secret ingredient to true freedom (as I've discovered over the years) — *discipline*.

Being disciplined gives you more freedom in everything you do. I talk about this more in future chapters.

☐ 8. The ability to adapt to change and embrace it.

I personally adore change, but I know many people who dislike it immensely. It puts them in a state of flux or doubt and fear.

Entrepreneurship and a location-independent lifestyle, require you to be even more flexible, adaptable, and open to change than normal. So embrace it!

If you think you can't, start by making micro-changes on a daily basis, like working from a different location, or working different hours, or changing one thing in your routine, and mixing it up.

Stay open to suggestions and opportunities. When you catch yourself feeling resistance, check in with yourself.

Are you just being stubborn or a bit scared, or is it a genuine fear — in which case, it's probably your intuition warning you for the right reasons.

Some of the best results or achievements I've had in life and business have come from being flexible and adaptable to change — like last minute paid speaking opportunities, fun adventure trips, and business partnerships.

I'd love for you to read through these key qualities again, and think about which ones resonate with you most.

Feel free to come up with your own qualities that you believe are necessary for you to make your own Freedom Plan a reality.

During the course of this book, you will inadvertently be working on these qualities almost all the time. You will develop these strengths as you go, so please keep working on the exercises that are part of every single chapter by going to the free companion video series at, thefreedomplan.co/start

Exercise your mindset muscles to feel more and more comfortable with your level of freedom and the lifestyle business you're growing.

Be Prepared To Be Challenged

Be prepared, as I said, to take two steps backward, instead of one step forward, at times. This is all about growth.

You are in Stage One of your Freedom Plan right now. It's about embracing the freedom mindset. This is the juicy stuff that's going to help you get rid of those limiting beliefs that you have.

This is the stage that's going to open your mind to the possibilities before you. This is the fun stage, and then the serious work starts.

So dream big, imagine what's possible, recognize what's been holding you back, and look at what is going to help you move forward.

Unload the outdated, limiting beliefs and ideas that are keeping you chained to your work, keeping you stuck at your current earning capacity, and leaving you feeling stressed and short on time, money and freedom.

Adopt the fresh and inspired mindset you need to go after your dreams and take charge of your future. Envision what you really want out of life, designing your ideal lifestyle, and making it a reality.

So, are you ready to choose freedom?

Choose. Simply choose to live your best possible life.

Do Not Settle For Mediocrity Any Longer

You have just one life, so make it the absolute best you can. Stop giving in to the excuses you've been making all along.

The fact that you are even reading this book right now, means that you have already made a choice that.

- You're worth it.

- You're investing in yourself.

- Now is the perfect time to make these changes in your life and business.

So thank you, thank you, thank you for making that decision.

Things are about to change for you if you're prepared to start taking action and define what your ideal lifestyle looks like.

One More Piece Of Advice

Focus on how good you're going to feel when you accept that life is in your control. And accept the wonderful power you have within you to accomplish great things in this world. I'm so excited for you!

Take all that you will learn during these next chapters and use it to continue creating your own Freedom Plan.

I know we have just started this journey, but you are with me for life, right?

What You Learned In This Chapter:

- In this chapter you learned how to apply the Sisson SMILE formula to your own life and business.

- You learned the 8 qualities you'll need to be a Freedomist. Go back and tick the boxes next to the qualities you have, so you know which ones you need to work on.

3

CREATING AND DESIGNING YOUR PERFECT DAY

Imagine waking up in a sunlit house, overlooking the ocean, surrounded by native bush, and nothing but the sound of the waves and beautiful bird songs.

You get up as the sun rises, after an absolutely refreshing sleep and are now raring to make the most of this beautiful day.

You take your yoga mat out onto your deck, into the sunshine and fresh air.

Your adorable dog Kayla is patiently waiting for your morning walk along the beach together. You play fetch with her, throwing the Frisbee out to sea, delighting in her boundless enthusiasm to go out and get it, and bring it back, ready to go again.

Then you both carry on for a thirty minute power walk, while you listen to your guided meditation on your phone, which helps you focus on envisioning your day ahead and exactly how you want it to look, feel and be like. You feel grounded and energized.

You arrive back in time to smell the delicious breakfast your personal chef Winston has made for you. You sit down at the table, after giving your partner a kiss, and settle down to a nutritious meal together — a tasty green smoothie and a delicious vegetable omelette.

You discuss your day ahead, your desires and intentions and then, after a lovely outdoor shower, you feel ready to start on your important work for the day around 10 am.

You've not been online at all, and have simply been present, enjoying the beauty of the day and company of your loved ones.

You settle into your beautiful minimalist office, on the top floor, with lush plants surrounding you and a clean white desk. You look out at the view of the ocean and breathe it all in, grateful for what you have.

This is pretty close to what I want one of my perfect days to look, feel, smell and sound like. What would your perfect day be like if you could describe it in detail?

Designing Your Perfect Day

I'd like to give you permission to take this time, right now, to let yourself drift away and daydream. Allow yourself to imagine exactly what your perfect day would look like.

Just let go and imagine how you'd spend your time, with who and where, from the moment you get up, to the moment you go to bed.

There's no need to limit yourself to only daydreaming about upcoming holidays, festivals, concerts or events you've had on your bucket list for years.

Tune into your happiest memories throughout life and the childlike wonder that most of us seem to have lost in our adulthood.

Treat today as if it's the start of your ideal your holiday, and let your imagination run wild!

Why you ask?

The thing is, and I have witnessed this happen in my own life and those of my Freedom Plan members, when you clearly state what your perfect day looks, feels, sounds and smells like, you actually move towards making it a reality.

It may be slow at first, but before you know it you're having more and more of your perfect days.

In my example above, you may think it sounds unrealistic. In fact, I've had plenty of emails from my clients before they take my course, saying it sounds like it's too good to be true and how could it possibly work?

Here's How:

If you live nowhere near a beach, you can improvise. Can you go to the local pool for a swim? Could you drive to a nearby river, lake, fountain or water display to get your fix of being around water? Most likely.

Or buy a big picture or poster of the ocean at sunrise, to put on your wall, so it's the first thing you see in the morning when you wake up.

Can you get up half an hour earlier to have breakfast in peace and your favourite meal with your partner or family? Yes, absolutely.

Could you afford to invest in a meal delivery service, where the food and recipes get delivered to you fresh each week saving you time, money and effort? Yes, you're worth it.

Could you clear a space or corner or even cupboard in your house, you can call your ideal working space. Paint it how you want, create a clean, cluttered and inspiring space that works for you? Yes.

Don't have your own place or there's just no space for such a thing? Then pick a cool local cafe that fits the bill or a rent a desk at a local coworking space.

Don't think you have thirty minutes of uninterrupted time in the morning for yoga?

Well then, start with five minutes. Surely, you're worth that much! You'll soon stretch it to ten or fifteen minutes or more as you realize how great it makes you feel.

Don't know how to do yoga and can't afford to take classes? No problem. There are a ton of free videos from instructors on YouTube - my favourite is *Yoga with Adrienne.*

There are a dozen or more, free and paid apps on Google Play and several in the iTunes store (like Down Dog or Daily Yoga), which you can use to do yoga from your own house.

Then there are cool services like Yogaglo.com, where you pay a small monthly subscription to get access to a huge range of instructors, through online videos, which you can play anytime, from ten minutes to ninety minutes, at all levels.

Still don't believe me?

Then perhaps it's time for a Freedom Mindset talk, where we tackle your beliefs and attitudes. As Nicola Rankin, habitsculptor.com and Freedom Plan alumni member stated.

> "I 'escaped' from my office job some years ago and made a (very brief) attempt at making a 'passive' income. I tried a couple of things, they didn't work out, and I felt uncomfortable about 'hustling.' I didn't realize it at the time, but finding something I am passionate about is extremely important to me, and the material I was reading didn't cover that at all.
>
> So I ended up doing freelance software development. I had escaped from the office, but was still tied to an hourly rate,

and doing work I no longer loved. To sort this out, I really needed to work on my mindset and point it towards freedom, rather than, security.

It's not enough to be able to work from anywhere. If you are doing something that you don't love, or are chained to an hourly rate, it still sucks. Well, better than working 9-5 in an office for sure, but NOT ENOUGH!

Freedom means, doing what you love just as much as doing it from wherever you like."

When I did my perfect day exercise, I realised there was nothing stopping me from making my days a bit more perfect right now.

It's amazing how just getting clear on what you really want, makes it so much easier to make it happen.

In 2017, I committed to getting the bulk of my work done in the mornings so my afternoons involved more free time. And to make sure it absolutely happens, I scheduled one afternoon off per week to go to the beach. As a result I did a fabulous job of working and playing over that summer.

In fact I worked (and played) from:

- A fabulous house-sitting job on the South Coast of Wellington.

- Kimi Ora Eco Resort in Kaiteriteri — this is a great find. Although, it's in a tiny little town at the top of the South Island, it has great wifi as well as a pool, spa, and massage service, and it's just a 15-minute walk to the beach. I would love to have stayed for longer!

- Nelson, house-sitting again in the inner city this time, so lots of walking around the river, parks, and of course, cafes.

It's not that I've never done this sort of thing before, it's that I'm enjoying it so much more.

Most of the work I'm doing is still for my 'day job.' But I'm comfortable now that my lifestyle is evolving in the direction that I have envisioned it in my 'perfect day' and in my 'Freedom Map.'

David Harder had this to say about doing the perfect day exercise.

> "I wrote furiously, describing the perfect day of my life. Pictures coming together, reinforcing the narrative with panoramic vistas of the description.
>
> My fingers flying on the keys, as I began to see in cinematic color, exactly how I wanted my day to look. What my body and mind experienced as I woke up, what the wood of the chair felt like as I sat at breakfast… the whole day rolling out like a perfect movie picture.
>
> Production, direction, acting; all coming together to create an Oscar performance."

In Vishen Lakhiani's book, '*The Code of the Extraordinary Mind*,' he talks about how our careers, our love lives, our happiness, our financial standing and our health, are all in conditions that are pretty inadequate. He writes.

> "People sometimes have to take jobs they dislike in order to make ends meet. They have to live in places they wouldn't choose because it's all they can afford at the time or they have family responsibilities.
>
> But there's a big difference between bending to life's necessities and blindly accepting that you must live your life according to preconceived rules.
>
> One of the keys to being extraordinary is knowing what rules to follow and what rules to break. Outside the rules of physics and the rules of law, all other rules are open to questioning.

Our beliefs about life, love, work, parenting, our bodies, and our self-worth. What you think and believe about the world shapes who you are and your experiences of the world around you.

Change your accepted models of reality and dramatic changes will happen in your world."

As another of my Freedom Plan Alumni members, Rob Garrett, robofficeninja.com says.

"For a few years, I have wanted a freedom lifestyle and attempted to come up with and implement business ideas. They never got very far, and it wasn't until I actively worked on changing my mindset and lifestyle that things are now on the way.

Sometimes, you just have to take a leap. I resigned from my job, as I know if I stayed there, 'just one more month,' it would turn into another month, another quarter, and another year.

It is scary, but there are other options, like doing part-time work initially or asking to adjust your hours or days at your current job.

Now, as a result of taking the leap, I'm happier than ever. In my life, I have implemented new routines, and these daily habitual changes have had a positive impact on my mindset. I started listening to business and lifestyle podcasts, exercising daily, drinking green smoothies, keeping a gratitude journal, and trying to be more mindful."

Next up is Sif Traustadóttir, Veterinarian sifthevet.com, talking about how the perfect day exercise helped her.

"I was stuck in a rut and heading into a midlife crisis, when I decided to change my life completely and travel in a campervan with my dog, for six months.

After going to your retreat, Natalie, I realised, having an online income that would allow me to live anywhere I wanted, really was a possibility and not just a pipe dream.

I found that making my first dollars online in my business was really important for my mindset — thinking it could work and validating my idea."

Now Sif owns a small house in Italy and enjoys the vita bella, going to Rome to catch up with friends or on trips to explore the Italian countryside and cuisine. All this, while helping dog owners live in more harmony with their beloved pooch, through her courses and online membership.

Or Mirian Bocija Sanchez, Career and Life Integration Coach at mirianbsanchez.com

"The Perfect Day was an exercise that gave me lots of clarity about why I'm building the business I'm building.

I always knew I loved surfing and the ocean and wanted to spend more time with the people I love, but they were just things that kept popping into my head without any real structure.

This exercise put all the pieces together. It became very clear to me the type of business and lifestyle I want.

I still don't have that lifestyle every day of my life, but since the exercise, more and more often, I live days like that one described in the exercise. And I won't stop until that becomes a daily reality.

I have printed my perfect day PDF presentation out with images, and it is in a folder on my bedside table. Now and again, I read it. Other times, I integrate the presentation into my meditation.

In those moments, when I feel confused about my business or my life, I always come back to the Perfect Day. It gets me back on track. It cuts off all the options that are making me confused and are not contributing towards that day."

So there you have it. What are you waiting for? Your perfect day is yours to design. It will serve you throughout the rest of this book, and for the entirety of your life.

It will be your muse when you need to remember why you're doing what you're doing, and it will be your guide when you veer off track from your Freedom Plan.

What You Learned In This Chapter:

- How to use the Perfect Day tool to make your dream life a reality.

- The power of visualization to get the results you want

Get your free Perfect Day template at thefreedomplan.co/start as part of the free companion video series.

STAGE 2

FREEDOM BUSINESS

4

USING YOUR UNIQUE SUPERPOWERS TO DESIGN YOUR FREEDOM BUSINESS

You may be thinking that your perfect day, from the previous chapter, is so far from where you are now, that it will never become a reality.

Especially if you are struggling in your business and not getting the results you want or if it constantly feels like a slog.

But that is a sure sign that you and your business are not in FLOW.

Flow is that 'magical' state when things feel natural and effortless. When you're in flow, you feel like you're in control and can make things happen easily, even while facing new challenges.

That's what having a freedom based business is all about — FLOW.

But what gets YOU into flow, may be totally different from other business owners, even if they are in the same industry or have a very similar business.

To make sure your perfect day is really *yours*, and to experience flow on a daily basis, you need to truly embrace your personal and entrepreneurial superpowers in everything you do.

In life this means focusing on what brings you joy, makes you energized and gives you purpose.

In work, it means designing your business in a way that focuses on your innate talents and delegate the activities that slow you down, sap your energy or make you feel like you're working in a 'job.'

Luckily for you, there are a few tests and assessments that will help you discover your superpower, and know whether the business you've set up is aligned with your strengths and personality.

The following are the ones I most recommend that have helped me and my clients greatly.

I will caveat, that no test can ever be a completely accurate summary of who you are - you are unique. Use these as *guiding* tools, not as your new found identity!

Wealth Dynamics

Wealth Dynamics is a personality profiling test designed by Roger Hamilton, that helps you put your finger on what your entrepreneurial superpower is, and then apply it to build your business, your team and your wealth.

It gives you insight into exactly what you should be focusing on, what activities you're best at, which areas you excel in, and what you absolutely should NOT be doing when it comes to work!

When you do the test you will discover which of the eight entrepreneurial profile types you are: Creator, Star, Supporter, Deal Maker, Trader, Accumulator, Lord or Mechanic.

You can do the paid test right now at the thefreedomplan.co/start / superpower

It will help you uncover the best business for your profile type and give you permission to say no to things that get you out of flow. When you do this, your fulfillment and effectiveness go up, and your stress and struggle go down.

For example, I'm a 'Star' profile. If I want to remain in flow and maximize my entrepreneurial superpowers, I focus on...

- Putting my voice into and shining light onto 'projects.'

- Blue-sky thinking and kickstarting projects.

- Marketing and promotions.

- Speaking on stage and sharing a big message.

- Working with a variety of people in large groups and platforms.

- Creating and curating unique courses and experiences.

If I focus on the following things instead, which I find challenging, I'll feel drained and out of alignment.

- Financial details and planning.

- Repetitive work.

- Detailed and ongoing implementation of projects.

- Lengthy research and analysis.

- Project management.

- Customer service activities.

That is why too much one-on-one coaching felt like a drain on my energy, although I loved my clients. Now, I choose selective mentoring of just a few clients who I see great potential in, and invest in companies and advise them on an ongoing basis.

And while I love doing my financials to understand my numbers and enjoy financial revenue projections and launch calculations, too much of that work depletes me.

However, starting new initiatives and businesses is my happy zone. My podcast, vlog and speaking engagements, allow me to be in flow and shine the spotlight on others.

This is in complete contrast to my dear friend Osmaan Sharif, a Performance and Mindset Coach and certified Wealth Dynamics consultant, who like me, also helps entrepreneurs grow their businesses, but in a different way.

At RapidTransformation.co.uk he coaches and mentors entrepreneurs by working closely with them on a one-to-one basis and also with ongoing group coaching programs and running repeat workshops.

For a 'Trader,' his winning strategies are more focused around.

- Getting down to the detail and focusing on implementation.

- Customer care and nurturing longer term relationships.

- Market research and seeing what other people miss.

- Focusing on 'trading' services or products *(often those created by others)*.

In contrast, the types of activities that would get him feeling out of flow would be.

- Creative design — starting from a blank canvas.

- Constant variety or ever-changing programs.

- System design and strategy.

- Innovative marketing campaigns.

This just goes to show that if we were to follow the design of each other's businesses, we'd feel out of flow, as if we were forcing our feet into the wrong pair of shoes. But when we work together, we combine our superpowers for even more impact.

There have been countless examples of when we've worked with business owners who had businesses that were designed in a way that wasn't supporting their entrepreneurial superpower.

Once they see this and shift to a business model, where they can play to their strengths more, it's transformative.

I also have each new team member take this assessment and then tell them how about how they can get in flow, and how they will fit and work with the team.

The Four Tendencies

Designed by bestselling author Gretchen Rubin, who focuses on happiness, habits and human behaviour, this free personality framework distinguishes how we respond to expectations.

Both *outer* expectations (a deadline, a "request" from a sweetheart) and *inner* expectations (write a novel in your free time, keep a New Year's resolution).

According to Gretchen, your response to expectations may sound slightly obscure, but it turns out to be very, very important.

The four profile categories are as follows:

- **Upholders** respond readily to outer and inner expectations (Gretchen is 100% an Upholder and so am I)

- **Questioners** question all expectations; they'll meet an expectation if they think it makes sense--essentially, they make all expectations into inner expectations

- **Obligers** meet outer expectations, but struggle to meet expectations they impose on themselves

- **Rebels** resist all expectations, outer and inner alike

You can take the free quiz at gretchenrubin.com/take-the-quiz

What I like about it is that the Tendencies do overlap, so each Tendency shares aspects with other Tendencies, although you can't be a mix.

As Gretchen states, to be an Upholder is not to be an Obliger. To be a Questioner is not to be a Rebel. While Upholders and Obligers both respond readily to outer expectations, it's how they respond to inner expectations that distinguishes them.

Similarly, Questioners and Rebels both resist outer expectations; it's how they respond to inner expectations that distinguishes them. And so on.

It's made me realize why I have a tendency for action and why I am true to my word - if I say I will do something I will damn well do it. The same thing applies to when I give my word to a friend or peer, and why integrity is my number one value.

It's helped me to run crowdfunding campaigns, write books, raise money for charities, go on daring adventures and create and launch numerous courses and products.

My friend Julie Treanor, a Leadership Coach for entrepreneurs, who I've run joint mentoring and mastermind workshops with, is a total rebel.

She sometimes won't even want to take her own advice, even though she's excellent at giving it! She's also not afraid to ask the hard questions or challenge people.

I enjoy partnering with her because our combined tendencies are complementary to how we both approach and perceive situations, and our clients challenges.

This framework is also helpful for relationships with your family and loved ones too. Plus you can read Gretchen's book The Four Tendencies, that goes much deeper into how this framework can affect your life and work.

CliftonStrengths 34

Don Clifton's strengths-based assessment is an essential test if you want to discover your strengths and play to them in life and business, like how you can best empower yourself, your team and or set and achieve goals.

If you want to stop trying to be more of who you're not, and start focusing on what naturally makes you powerful and unique, then the CliftonStrengths 34 test will be right up your alley.

I first came across this 8 years ago when I read the Book StrengthsFinder 2.0 (which this test used to be called). It helped shine a light on my personal strengths that I could apply to my work, relationships and also how I showed up in a team and, back then, as a budding leader.

It's based on 40 years of research and extremely credible. Many organizations, teams and individuals use this test to maximize their potential.

You can buy the test here gallupstrengthscenter.com/

I re-did the test in late 2017 and two of my top 5 strengths have changed. The new results helped me focus on where I should be putting my energies - both personally and professionally.

Here are mine. If you've met me, watched my videos or heard me speak, they will probably make a lot of sense to you:

1. **Woo**: People who are especially talented in the Woo theme love the challenge of meeting new people and winning them over. They derive satisfaction from breaking the ice and making a connection with another person.

2. **Activator**: People who are especially talented in the Activator theme can make things happen by turning thoughts into action. They are often impatient.

3. **Communication:** People who are especially talented in the Communication theme generally find it easy to put their thoughts into words. They are good conversationalists and presenters.

4. **Positivity:** People who are especially talented in the Positivity theme have an enthusiasm that is contagious. They are upbeat and can get others excited about what they are going to do.

5. **Relator:** People who are especially talented in the Relator theme enjoy close relationships with others. They find deep satisfaction in working hard with friends to achieve a goal.

I chuckle out loud at how true these are for me. Try it for yourself and more importantly acknowledge and use your strengths on a daily basis to really show up in the world. You can uncover all 34 of your strengths if you want to go even deeper.

Which leads me to the final test I recommend.

How the World Sees You (Fascination Advantage)

Sally Hogshead's Fascination Advantage assessment identifies how you best gain attention and influence people with your personality and gifts. It's based on six years of research and 1 million participants.

When you buy the book, How the World Sees You, you get a code that gives you access to take the assessment or you can simply buy it here https://www.howtofascinate.com/

This takes about twenty minutes. Once you've taken the assessment you receive information about your hidden talents, your highest worth and your unrealised potential. In other words your primary and secondary advantages as well as your archetype (one of forty nine).

For me it's been most helpful for positioning my personal brand and understanding what's unique about me, and how to emphasize that to best effect.

Rather than getting stuck on my view of the world, and how I see others, the Fascination Report lets me know how clients and coworkers see me, at my best.

You can find out how you are most likely to make a brilliant first impression, how your personality adds value to team and better ways to communicate with people using your unique advantages.

If you're curious, the world sees me as *The Victor*

1. Respected

2. Results Oriented

3. Competitive

Bang on!

My primary advantage is **Prestige** - which is my most effective mode of communication. When I communicate with this I'm at my most fascinating and influential apparently!

My secondary advantage is **Power**, it's my second highest mode of communication and describes how my personality is most likely to add value and when I use it I come across as more confident and authentic.

Sally has also create a Team Fascination Advantage framework and does a particularly good job of detailing out your results, what they mean and how to best use them.

The trick to any assessment, framework, test or quiz is to apply it in the best possible way to your situation now, and revisit it often.

Every quarter, or at least annually, I will revisit my results and take notes to better understand myself and how I'm adding the most value to the world, or what I need to improve or focus on.

Manifest Your Dreams and Change Your Beliefs

Along with taking these tests, I've read my fair share of 'self-help' books and applied these learnings to my daily life. It has made a huge difference to who I am and how I behave.

The most significant difference has been to my mindset and my ability to reframe, even when the going gets tough.

Two of the most influential books I've read were, 'Awaken the Giant Within' from Tony Robbins and Napoleon Hill's 'Think and Grow Rich.'

The first book introduced me to Neuro Linguistic Programming (NLP) and how to apply it to change long-held beliefs that weren't serving me.

The latter one showed me the power of visualization combined with taking action, and the results I could achieve.

Every time I 'do more work on myself' and put aside time to challenge my assumptions, beliefs, and attitudes, I see massive personal growth and positive changes in my life.

Once I catch those stories I'm telling myself or any negative talk, at the moment, I can switch it and reframe it to work for me and empower me. Life gets so much better as you find tools that work for you to improve your mindset.

Yet, no one teaches this stuff in school or college and it's rarely discussed in the workplace. As an entrepreneur, it's probably one of the most important investments you can make in your education and yourself.

Look at the word **'be-LIE-f'** — there's a big fat 'lie' in the middle of it.

But the way your mind works is that it takes on all beliefs you've accepted *(either willingly or without realization)* and sees them as being 100% true.

The scary thing is that these beliefs run on autopilot and shape how you think, feel, and act. You don't even realize it most of the time, because they run in the background!

Here's a five step exercise that you can do to create a rapid transformation in those beliefs that no longer serve you.

I've seen how powerful this technique is when Osmaan shares this belief busting session, as a guest coach on my Escape To Freedom retreats.

Belief Buster Exercise

Ask yourself and write down answers to the following.

Step 1. What are some of my beliefs that are limiting me or holding me back?" (*'I'm not good enough to .....; 'It's too risky to .....'; 'Who am I to ....?')*

Step 2. Choose one and then rate that belief on how much it currently feels true to you. 0 = Not true at all, to 10 = 100% solid fact.

Step 3. Now, it's time to use the power of your unconscious mind to put them under the spotlight and challenge them using these five belief busting questions.

1. How has this limiting belief held me back in the past?

2. What has it stopped me from achieving or doing?

3. What could I lose if I ultimately don't let go of it now?

4. Why am I totally committed to letting it go now?

5. When did I take on this belief?

Step 4. Tune back in and see how that belief now feels out of a 10. You should have noticed that it doesn't feel as real anymore — like you've popped a balloon and it starts to deflate.

Step 5. Put all your limiting beliefs in the hot seat and take them through those five steps again.

After Freedom Plan Alumni Member, Jo Bendle, a Productivity Coach for Female Entrepreneurs at jobendle.co.uk experienced this powerful exercise at my retreat, she shared this on her blog:

> "For context, if you don't know me, as of March 2015 I have been 100% location independent (so I have no home base, I travel the world with my laptop).
>
> Costa Rica sounded like a gorgeous destination to work from. And so off I went. Turns out it was hugely transformational and confronting too!
>
> It all started whilst being in an absolutely beautiful area of the world, totally loving my business, working with the most incredible women...and wondering why the hell was I still feeling so UNFULFILLED.
>
> Have you ever achieved a big dream and then thought to yourself, hang on a minute...
>
> "Is this it??"
>
> I even feel bad saying it, people would pay money for what I had created and I was feeling like — hey, where's the brilliant stuff I was expecting?

I did the work, I got here — now why doesn't it feel amazing??! That wasn't part of the deal.

Here I was, unfulfilled and feeling ready to tackle it once and for all.

That started some deep soul searching, lots of inner work. I tapped, I journaled, I meditated, and I wrote in my journal about what I was 'satisfied' with (proof to my mind that I wasn't unfulfilled) and bit by bit, things started to get clearer and clearer…or juicier and juicier.

I calmly allowed all the shifts and thoughts to come and go. I found it fascinating to watch what was coming up. Actually, it was super interesting to watch. I love this stuff even if it feels HARD at the time.

Every single day a new realization arrived in my journal. I have to say the hardest part of this whole process was getting started with the very first 'why do I feel unfulfilled' moment.

Because I didn't have the answer and it didn't make any sense.

From there it's just been a massively exciting unraveling of thoughts and beliefs that have been holding me back from playing a bigger game.

"I can't put my finger on it, I'm living my dream life and yet, I'm not happy.'

That was the journal entry where I started to dig a little deeper.

I was feeling pretty frustrated with myself too. I felt I wasn't giving it my all to the business, or my life. I was still playing it safe. I wasn't showing up properly. I was holding back.

I was holding back. Whoa. Why Jo?

One of my big fears is being average and mediocre, now, I can see I'm not those things, but my mind had decided that I was.

And I believed my mind. 100%.

And of course, my actions, meant I could keep proving my mind right.

And the a-ha moments just kept coming, the last one was about my choice of lifestyle. What started with a journal entry about feeling unfulfilled, has led me to my next mission and adventure, which feels very exciting.

Before I got to Costa Rica, I was in the resistance stage, so it was pretty clear something big was coming.

And it came!

Amazingly, now I don't feel unfulfilled.

I'm not blocked by limiting thoughts and beliefs. All the work and all the letting go has basically brought me to the next fork in the road.

In this moment, Jo made a big mindset shift that allowed her to move on to the next stage of her Freedom Plan. What do I want you to take away from all this?

Resistance and frustration are totally natural and part of the journey to living your best possible life.

Doing the inner work every day is imperative if you want to understand you, your desires, your motivations and your inner psyche.

Even if it's just five minutes writing down your gratitudes, asking yourself deep probing questions, or sitting with your emotions and watching them with curiosity.

If you do this regularly you'll experience real shifts and moments of epic clarity. You'll let go of limiting beliefs, irrational fears and rapidly accelerate your journey towards freedom!

What You Learned In This Chapter:

- How to tap into your entrepreneurial superpowers to get in flow and do more of the work you love.

- Four tests you can take to help you better understand yourself and your unique talents, skills and strengths, as well as how to relate to others.

- Why your business model needs to align with who you are to succeed.

- How to use the Belief Buster exercise to stop sabotaging yourself.

5

MONETIZING YOU AND BUILDING YOUR EXPERT PLATFORM

As you're probably beginning to realize, there's no cookie-cutter approach to freedom. If you want your ideal freedom business and lifestyle, then you have to chart your own path.

The great news is, you are uniquely you and there is NO ONE else out there like you. That's your *unfair advantage,* which you need to capitalize on.

How? By monetizing yourself.

You know the values you need to be a Freedomist, you've learned what your entrepreneurial superpowers are, and you've hopefully started shifting your mindset and unblocking your limited beliefs.

So how do you then take that a step further and turn your talents and skills into multiple revenue streams that are all aligned with your purpose?

Well, how about I share a story because there's no better way to get to the core of the matter and understand it, than a good ol' explanation you can resonate with.

What follows is the story of how I combined my eight years of experience in the corporate world, my time as a Tech startup Cofounder, and my seven years running my own business to end up where I am today.

This example will make it clear that every single experience you've had in life, every single thing you've done, makes up ALL of you, and in turn, makes up all your business and lifestyle opportunities.

The Birth of Brand 'Natalie Sisson'

Ever since I was two years old, when my parents took me on my first overseas trip, I've had the travel bug, instilled by them.

I grew up enjoying many family trips overseas, for which I am still truly grateful. Back then, kids under twelve years flew free, so that helped!

Exposure to new places, cultures, and languages, made me a more curious child. As a result, at school, I threw myself into a variety of activities.

I wrote for the school magazine, I was on several sports teams — touch rugby, netball, tennis, cricket, and I coached a junior netball team. I learned Japanese and German, I sang in the choir, learned piano, and I was always up for an adventure and volunteering for new things.

By my final year at school, I had collected way too many badges on my school blazer. A few years ago, Mum pulled it out of a box and handed it to me, and we both laughed at how many extra-curricular activities I was involved in.

I'm not sure how I managed it all!

Surprisingly, nothing has changed. I adore living life to the fullest. I thrive on variety and challenge.

I have a diverse social circle of friends from around the world. I still love to travel, I'm continuing to learn languages, I love to play tennis and Ultimate Frisbee, go sailing, surfing and skiing, do boxing and Crossfit to name a few.

I also loved journaling as a child and did this religiously for nine consecutive years. Now, I have a stack of diaries in boxes I look forward to reading over the coming years.

The point of this story is to show you that the *signs* were there early on; that I loved writing, storytelling, and charting my life adventures.

When I went to university, I did two degrees in just four years. One was a Bachelor in Tourism and Service Management and the other was a Bachelor in Information Systems, so basically, the two things I focused on with The Suitcase Entrepreneur!

I'm thankful for the many and varied corporate jobs I have had. I was notorious for interviewing well for jobs that were above my current experience level.

I'd get really good at what I did, master the skills quickly, then get bored, quit and go traveling...until I ran out of money and had to come back and get another job. This happened over and over again.

I amassed a wide range of skills over those eight years, in a variety of different sectors, including healthcare, FMCG (fast moving consumer goods), education, and safe gaming!

These have become extremely handy, as I've built my business, including brand development, product launches, event management, customer relations, business development, team management and so much more.

I think you're starting to get the picture, right?

The sum of ALL of me, made me into who I am today and set me up for my dream role as The Suitcase Entrepreneur.

Fast forward to when I started my business in April 2010, and realised , looking back a few years later, that I had combined all those fields of interest together to form my perfect lifestyle business.

My love for learning and educating others, writing, producing, creating, and of course, travel and adventure, all got woven into my life and business.

Had I known this when I was a kid, had I looked at all the things that I did during my lifetime when I was younger, I might have started my business before I even went to University or instead of it.

Would I have been ready then? Possibly not. All the great skills and experience that followed, also set me up for the first business I built.

My Exact Path To Monetizing Myself

As I shared in my TEDx talk, after eight years in the corporate world, honing my skills in branding, marketing and business development, I quit my job in July 2008 when enough was enough. I was through with being in a soul sucking environment with layers of hierarchy, egos and bureaucracy.

I took a leap of faith and headed off to Canada to play World Championship Ultimate Frisbee and start my own business in Vancouver.

I met my business partner at one of the many networking events I attended and we co-founded a technology startup Connection Point Systems, and built Fundrazr, a Facebook fundraising app, that is still going strong today.

That was in September 2008, a mere two months after arriving in Canada. I learned a lot of lessons along the way and so here they are.

Step 1: Build Your Knowledge And Core Foundational Skills

I spent eighteen months helping build our company and FundRazr. I learned so much during that time.

I cut my teeth in the entrepreneurial world, I helped raise an investment round, hired team members, worked with our developers to build our app and miraculously watched as we built an entire business from scratch, with zero budget, using social media.

Among the many hats I wore as an entrepreneur, it was my responsibility to learn and understand how to use social media to grow our business.

I threw myself into it. Consuming blogs, books, videos and attending a few online events to learn more. During that time, I started blogging at *WomanzWorld*.

That blog became my entire business, which I renamed a year later to, *The Suitcase Entrepreneur.*

That blog soon became much more of a passion to me, than the business we started, it tapped into my entrepreneurial superpowers and put me in a state of flow.

So in 2010, I left our company with just my blog and minimal savings to start my business.

The trouble is I didn't really know what my business was. All I had was this little blog with a very small audience and a lot of skills behind me.

Step 2. Own It

It turns out that using social media to grow your business, is an area that I was very adept at by that stage. It was something entrepreneurs needed to learn and understand and as a result they would happily pay for training.

I used it to find our customers, build our credibility, promote and market our app, get press attention and put out all the content designed to build our brand and get leads and new customers.

Combine that with years of marketing and business development skills, including launching products in different industries, running events and growing the business.

People sat up and noticed in Vancouver and I started to develop a bit of a reputation in this area. I was using my personal blog to share tips and tactics about social media more regularly as well.

Step 3. Work It

Upon this realization, I went all in, publishing a 12-part blog post series on using social media on my blog, which got a great amount of attention.

It took a lot of effort and a long time to write such in depth posts, but I was fully committed to share my knowledge while it was 'hot.'

I then turned that series of blog posts, into a free eBook '*The Social Media Workout for Entrepreneurs*' that I gave away when people opted in to join my email list.

Note: It took me six months of blogging, before realizing I was missing out on a huge opportunity to build my list. I had no way for people to opt in and receive updates from me when they really wanted to. Please don't make that mistake.

Slowly, but surely, that list and my website traffic grew by a couple of hundred to a thousand or so people. Then a few months after parting ways, amicably with my business partner Daryl in April 2010, I realised I had better put these skills and talents to the test pronto, or risk going broke in a month or two.

I mean all this blogging and free content was building loyalty, trust and my reputation, but I had no money coming in at all!

Step 4. Put a Price On It

I brainstormed what I could offer and ended up putting myself out there in a way that both scared and excited me. I advertised my *Social Media Bootcamp* workshop, held over two full days and priced at CAN$1500.

I tapped into government funding so businesses could come for much less, but I'd get the full payout.

This was my first live event and a big deal for me. Luckily, I stepped into my 'Star' profile and it was a hit.

I ended up selling out not one, but three workshops and going from broke to US$15,000 in less than a month.

That felt so good. Especially as a few months earlier, I was seriously contemplating giving up and thinking I wasn't cut out for business.

It turned out to be the first ah-ha moment I had, where I realised I could technically take this business on the road.

Yes, I'd be leaving behind my well established network in Vancouver, but I had my online community and there was no reason, I argued, to stay put in one place when I could take this business with me in a suitcase!

How you ask?

I did this by turning my Social Media Bootcamp workshop into an online program.

I flew from Vancouver to Las Vegas to hang out with friends and attend a conference or two, including BlogWorld, where I met many amazing people I'm still friends with to this day and really improved my blogging skills.

While in Vegas I spent over forty long hours recording videos in Camtasia, a video editing software, by speaking over the top of all my powerpoint presentations I'd used in the workshop and essentially 'teaching' the workshop all over again.

At the end of it, I had hours and hours of content in video and audio format, plus PDF handouts.

Armed with this I marketed it to my community through my blog, social media, email and my first ever webinar. By this stage I was in San Francisco staying at a friends.

The night I ran it I was sick, and had almost lost my voice, but was determined to show up. One hundred people had registered and thirty people showed up.

I made one sale of USD$297. And was over the moon.

Sure, it wasn't a spectacular result for over forty hours of work, but the first dollars you make online, you never forget.

Why? Because they validate that someone is prepared to pay for your knowledge in the format and package you've presented to them.

From there I took off to Buenos Aires, Argentina to test this further and the rest is history. Ever since, I've been roaming the world creating products and programs that meet the needs of my wonderful community, blog readers and podcast listeners.

Step 5. Stay Hungry

It doesn't end there. As it happens in life, things got worse before they got better. I didn't make a ton more sales from that program - certainly not enough to live off.

So I had to come up with more revenue streams. By now I realised, that people wanted interaction, coaching and hand holding.

Enter the '*Social Media Club.*' A simple premise of a password protected Wordpress page, where each month I released a short thirty minute training video on the latest and greatest updates in Social Media the members should know about.

They also got access to a lively Facebook group and a Q+A call each month. For $19 dollars it was a steal and I had around one-hundred members at its peak. This provided a great recurring income, at a time when consistent revenue was lacking.

It was also a simple setup that had very few barriers to me delivering it.

I think we have a tendency, as we learn more and become more sophisticated in our businesses, to over complicate things. Simple and elegant always works well for your customers.

Still, that club wasn't really bringing in enough to cover my business running costs or my lifestyle, which was minimal at best.

So I had to create something else. Here's what I did.

Step 6. Rinse and Repeat

I looked to my audience and paid close attention to what they were always asking me questions about - the comments on the blog, the repeating patterns of interaction on social media, and I had an epiphany.

Another one of my superpowers was to make the complex simple, especially when it came to using tools and technology.

Therefore, after some research and priming my community, I went to work on creating '*The Ultimate Toolkit for Evolutionary Entrepreneurs.*'

I researched and tested the best of the best tools in different areas of business like sales, marketing, finance etc and shared them in a beautifully designed eBook (that cost over $2,000 to design) for $47 dollars.

I also offered a Premium version, this included the eBook and an online component and created a mini course site to host video training and further resources, which dug in deeper to some areas and provided email access to me for questions. This was $197.

I put a LOT more effort into the launch. I studied Jeff Walker and a number of other 'gurus' in the online marketing world, to decipher what they were doing, every step of the way to be successful during their launches, and I emulated it.

I'm not going to lie, I thought I had it all figured out. I was very proud of what I put out. And the launch was a flop. The first 24 hours....silence.

I distinctly remember throwing myself on the bed in my studio apartment in Buenos Aires wailing, " I don't get it, what more do I need to do, why is this launch such a failure?"

I cried for a good hour and held my own pity party for one. Then, slowly but surely, people responded and I started to make sales. Then more and over the coming weeks, more still.

That product existed for a further two years before I retired it and it made me around $25,000 dollars all together.

Step 7. Repeat Step 6

No seriously. I think most people underestimate how much hustle and creativity an entrepreneur needs to pour into their business in the first few years to TRULY get traction and get somewhere.

Strategic hustle is where it's at.

Create, test, validate and fail fast, then do it again, but better, every time.

Here's another example. Eighteen months after my first successful blog post series, I wrote and published the *BYOB Build Your Online Business* series.

To date, I think this is some of my best work. I poured every ounce of knowledge I'd learned over two years of running my business into this.

People loved it. My list grew, my blog traffic grew, sales of my existing products increased and there was a demand for more.

I think I had finally cracked it.

I took this blog post series and turned it into another beautifully designed eBook of the same name, with templates and checklists. I put it up for sale, after some strategic launch marketing, for $37 dollars.

I went further and made a premium version for $57 dollars that included a short one hour group coaching call with me, and then, became a link future customers could access within the book.

I created an audio version for fun. I sold that for $19 dollars. To my surprise it sold well!

Then I followed the 'bundling' methodology I'd been learning by modeling others online, where I priced the book and audio at $47 dollars. That became a hit.

Then, around four months later, I took that book and created the next in the BYOB series, called *Am I Your Customer.'*

Essentially, I'd seen a specific need for breaking down how to understand who your ideal avatar is and then go about better understanding their needs so you can market to them with more success, as well as create and validate solutions they actually need and will buy.

This was also priced at $37 dollars. Or you could buy both for $57 dollars.

Another six months later and I produced the third book in the BYOB series, *'Build Your Own Lucrative Sales Funnel.'* Again, this was an area people were falling down on that was holding them back.

Building a successful sales funnel is critical for growing and automating your business.

I was not an expert in sales funnels at this stage, I'm still not. It's a continuing area of learning and improving, optimizing and testing and I love it.

But I knew more than most of my audience at the time, and that's all you need. If you can show value, and help them make more sales and get more leads, that's invaluable and something people will pay for.

Collectively over the years I made over $120,000 from these eBooks, until I pulled them from my online shop in late 2015, to simplify my offerings and make way for new ones.

But it doesn 't need to stop there. Keep evolving and creating.

I turned this book series into the BYOB World Tour and taught the content of these ebooks in physical workshops in New Zealand, Australia, Japan, Canada, United Kingdom and the United States.

I limited these workshops to twelve people, to keep it intimate and ensure ample practical learning time, although Melbourne had eighteen people book in for it!

I charged US$500 a head for a full day, plus my digital books were included as added value.

While I didn't technically need to do this, my online offerings were set up in a way to give me more freedom and revenue for far less work than organizing events, I was already traveling to all of these places, and there is nothing like the personal touch.

More importantly, I realised I most value in person connections with my community, which I wasn't getting from my online interactions.

That's why in Chapter 2, I go over the SMILE formula and apply it to myself on a regular basis, and in Chapter 4, I cover knowing your entrepreneurial superpowers.

Your work has to align with your values and purpose.

Step 8. Align Your Vision

I share all this so you can see how much strategic hustling I had to do to get to where I needed to be. With each and every action I took, I created more momentum and opportunity to expand on what I already had. It began to snowball!

I also listened and learned from my audience, building and creating products that they were actually *asking for*, not that I thought would be cool to work on and release.

These days the 'gurus' will tell you how you can quickly get rich if you just follow their formula. Each person is trying to teach the method they mastered to build a profitable business. While they will have some merit, they won't usually work for you.

The thing is, as we went over in Chapter 4, your unique superpowers will work best in a custom designed business model that suits your skills, strengths and tendencies, not theirs.

All of these revenue streams I created, were in alignment with superpowers *and* my lifestyle vision, which meant that none of them required me to be doing anything in person (unless I chose to, like I did with my workshops), or full time.

Most of my work became automated over time and delivered in the cloud instantly to my lovely customers without my input. I designed my business for everyday freedom.

I put in massive initial effort upfront, to set up and create residual recurring income streams for years to come, so I could go on to travel to 70+ countries, live out of a suitcase and bounce around the world for 6+ years!

I could go offline for days or even weeks at a time and know everything was taken care of.

By year two I had started hiring a small, but nimble virtual team of part time contractors, to help me do that even more. This took the pressure off me. Bliss.

I built a multiple six-figure business by teaching what I know, monetizing myself, being ridiculously helpful, very accessible and transparent.

By taking action to create and produce things that people actually find valuable, useful and worth paying for, I've helped them go on to enjoy their own freedom plan journey.

You can and should do this too, on your own terms, with your own sweet spot, for your own mission-driven purpose.

Step 9. Seize the Opportunity

Along with all this goodness came paid speaking opportunities, introductions to movers and shakers, invitations to events and conferences, from which great partnerships formed, including with my dear friend Natalie MacNeil.

We released WE Mastermind (Women Entrepreneurs' Mastermind) in 2012, a 12 week course teaching you how to launch online, which brought in multiple six figures between us over two years.

We added in physical retreats on cruise ships to destinations like the Caribbean, as a high ticket item to coach and teach motivated women entrepreneurs in person.

My Amazon bestselling book, *The Suitcase Entrepreneur* came out of all the knowledge and understanding I'd gleaned from my BYOB series and years of one-on-one and group coaching.

I've been featured in incredible major press across the world and I've grown this business that I adored, while traveling the world, meeting the most awesome people and changing people's lives. I feel very blessed.

The world really is your oyster when you open your mind to what's possible and align it, once again, with how you want to live your life, and those perfect day moments you desire.

Creating Your Unique Freedom Business

My story is just one example of a route you can take to build your own Freedom Business based around YOU.

But there are hundreds of thousands of people who've gone off and figured out their own route, based on what they already know, the skills they already have and more importantly, the lifestyle they desire.

Let's dive into just a handful that I've discovered and researched for you in the next chapter.

What You Learned In This Chapter:

- The exact way in which I built my revenue streams from scratch.

- Nine key steps to take to monetise yourself using your sweet spot.

6

CHOOSING THE RIGHT REVENUE STREAMS FOR FINANCIAL FREEDOM

The purpose of this chapter is to help you identify your best path to monetization.

Now that you're armed with knowing your Entrepreneurial Superpowers, it makes sense to see if the revenue streams you currently have, or plan to introduce, are in fact in alignment with your profile, and your values.

If you want to succeed in making your Freedom Plan a reality, you have to make sure you structure your current or future revenue streams to serve your financial goals too.

For simplicity's sake I like to break revenue streams down into two methods.

1. Selling yourself, your services or products.

2. Selling other people's stuff.

You need to decide which of those suits you best, or you can combine them both, but bear in mind **the end goal is not to be self-employed, it's to run a business.**

I make this differentiation, as most people start their business trading time for money, and years after, are often stuck still doing that.

Now, this may be a necessity to get off the ground and bring in immediate income, but within twelve to twenty four months, you ultimately want to build a business - one that is not tied to you, your energy or your activity.

While I cover funnels and hiring in the upcoming chapters, you want to decide for yourself today what your freedom plan is.

Now, Let's Dive Into The Two Simplified Methods That You Can Change Or Swap To, At Any Time, To Suit Your Freedom Plan.

Method #1 is selling yourself

This is where you sell your knowledge and skills you've acquired in your lifetime and package it into products and services. This is one of the most natural ways to build a business that you love.

You start by marketing and selling yourself via social media, blogging, vlogging, podcasts, interviews, speaking and positioning yourself as the go-to person in your niche with free content and education people value.

From there you monetise yourself through your platform and create online and offline offerings, virtual or physical, that include one or more of the following.

- Online courses

- Digital products

- Books

- Coaching/ consulting*

- Group coaching/ training

- Workshops/ events

- Services*

- Speaking*

- Software products

- E-commerce

*Typically these activities will see you trading time for money.

As you grow and become more credible, so will your business.

I'm the perfect example of this, as someone with multiple revenue streams, and there are millions of other people doing the same. I'm about to introduce you to some of them and show you what's possible!

Jasper Ribbers Has Made A Lifestyle Business As An Airbnb Expert

In March 2010, Jasper gave up his finance career to pursue a lifelong dream to travel the world full-time. As he puts it, he left behind the lovely apartment, the fancy car and the big salary to go off and visit up to 75 countries (and counting).

To support himself, Jasper has been renting out his apartments on Airbnb. He became such a pro at it, figuring out the best way to maximize his listing, that he went on to position himself as an expert on Airbnb, after initially learning how to make money from it himself.

He also did this when the platform was still young, so he established his credibility fast before too many 'new players' came onto the scene.

Airbnb is personally one of my favourite tools in the world for finding great accommodation around the world in people's homes, apartments and houses. It lets you find accommodation, generally, for less money than you would pay for a hotel, and for a much more personal and authentic experience. It's also a platform that allows you to 'host' and rent out your own place too.

As a result Airbnb has created a whole community and economy of people who have realised that they can collectively share and rent their places, earn money from it, or travel the world and stay in amazing places.

Jasper's first Airbnb listing of his Amsterdam apartment in July 2012 met with excellent results.

> "I grossed 13,000 Euros for the six months I rented it out in that year, then 40,000 Euros in 2013 and over 50,000 Euros a year since then."

He's making much more money than if he had rented out his apartment to long term renters. In addition, he wouldn't have been able to stay in his home when he was back in Amsterdam.

> "I stayed in my house four to six weeks each year. The expenses totallled about a thousand Euros a month, including cleaning and check-ins, condo fees, bills, TV and internet. The value of the house was around 350,000."

Since 2014, his pre-tax return on investment has been almost 11%, which is great!

In June 2014, he took it further. He launched his Amazon book, *Get Paid for Your Pad* because he realised people wanted to know how to become successful at listing on Airbnb and there weren't any good resources out there.

The launch was incredibly successful, which helped position Jasper as the go-to expert on how to make the most of your Airbnb listing and create your own lifestyle of freedom.

Jasper was invited to the Airbnb headquarters, where he met with the founders, who support his work, and he's held workshops at the Airbnb Open, their yearly hosting event. He's been featured all around the web, including the prestigious NY Times.

He makes money from selling his book on Amazon and also has affiliate deals with Airbnb startups, like Everbooked, Beyond Pricing and Payfully, that all help you maximize your Airbnb listing and scheduling.

Along with the book launch, he started a weekly podcast, in which he interviews Airbnb hosts from all around the world. He also found sponsors that pay for the production costs of the podcast.

Jasper has since invested in short-term rental properties in Colombia, the Philippines and Thailand. He's documenting his experiences, which will form the foundation of his upcoming book on how to invest with the purpose of renting out on Airbnb.

Jasper is a good example of someone who took something, taught himself more about it and then started monetizing his expertise by teaching the information to others. As a result, he gets invited to speak at conferences around the world.

That's strategic hustling at its best!

Nora Dunn Does Financial Planning From The Road

While running her financial planning business in Toronto, Canada, Nora became increasingly aware that her lifelong dream to intensively travel the world, was actually slipping away.

So in 2006, she took the plunge and sold up and she has been traveling in a financially sustainable manner ever since.

She realised that the vital component of her happiness came through travel. Therefore, she set about building an income stream that would support her life of travel.

> "It dawned on me that my lifelong penchant for the written word could translate into an income earned around the world, with a little more than an internet connection and a laptop."

Nora used the proceeds from selling her former business, to fund the first two years of her travel - she budgeted $20,000 per year. While travelling, Nora has used her free time to set up her freelance writing career.

She took advantage of her early start in blogging as The Professional Hobo, which I love as a name, and has crafted a viable business by marrying her experience in full time travel and her previous career in finance.

> "I wrote for finance publications about travel and I wrote for travel publications about finance. On my website, I marry the two topics to teach people how to travel full-time in a financially sustainable way.
>
> It was a long, slow process to get it all going though. And given the blogging industry was still brand new at the time, I stumbled my way up the learning curve feeling very much like I was inventing the wheel by myself."

But as you can see, Nora has found her sweet spot for her own career, which is as she puts it, freelance writer and a blogger on travel, personal finance, and lifestyle design, which might seem random. Well, that's kind of what I do. But it's actually complementary.

As she pointed out...

- She is a concert pianist, which is good for typing.

- She is a sales person, which is good for creating compelling pitches to editors as well as telling good stories in her articles.

- She is a financial professional so she can write about finance and travel.

- She was an administrative assistant so she knows how to run a business.

- She is a skydiver so she has that sense of adventure for travel.

So you can see how she has combined all these things that she loves to do into her sweet spot.

Nora's annual earnings have ranged from $22,000 to $43,000. Although, she could easily earn more than that, she chooses to work less and focus extra time on her lifestyle and travels.

She documents her annual income and expenses every year on her blog, to demonstrate how her full-time travel lifestyle is financially sustainable.

> "One of the benefits of my nomadic existence in developing my writing career, was that I consistently found that the cost to travel full time has been less than the cost to live in one place. So in the years when I wasn't earning much from writing, I could still live quite happily on very little."

Paul And Sheryl Shard Get Paid To Sail The World

In 1989, when they had just turned 30, Paul and Sheryl set out on a two year sailing sabbatical that they had been saving for since high school.

They fell in love with the cruising lifestyle and found the money they'd saved would allow them to carry on traveling for a third year of cruising. They sailed over 20,000 nautical miles and visited 23 countries as a result.

Paul's background was in IT, but he freelanced as a photographer and videographer. Sheryl's background was in theatre and film. It just made sense that they'd document their adventures.

When they returned to Canada in 1992, they cut an hour documentary, *Call of the Ocean*, about their first trip and the Discovery Channel licensed it for their Search for Adventure series!

People loved it and wanted to see more and the rest is history.

They have now been sailing and living aboard for almost 30 years and have shot two series about the sailing life, Exploring Under Sail and Distant Shores.

Distant Shores is now in its 11th season, with 130 half-hour episodes and more to follow, when the Shards sail their new boat to the South Pacific. Television production is their main income.

Distant Shores is broadcast worldwide in twenty four languages and in six continents. The show is also available online as HD downloads on Vimeo and on DVD through their DistantShores.ca website.

> "We also have a YouTube Channel, which we have been building (now 40,000 subscribers) to extend our global reach which is an added source of income through monetization via ads and sponsorship."

Paul and Sheryl have now sailed over 100,000 miles, have made 8 ocean crossings , with a 9th on the way, and documented their travel experiences sailing to more than sixty countries and colonies around the Atlantic Ocean, Caribbean, Mediterranean, North Sea and Baltic Sea.

They sail about eight months of the year, while filming. The rest of the time they are working in the Shard Multimedia studio at home in Canada. This is where they do post-production on the shows they've just shot. They also conduct seminars at boat shows and yacht club events.

They also write for sailing publications and have written a best-selling book called, *"Sail Away! A Guide to Outfitting and Provisioning for Cruising,"* which is now being updated to its third edition.

Occasionally they host sail training weeks aboard their boat, for fellow sailors or those new to the lifestyle, who are hoping to do some long-distance travelingon their own boats in the future, especially, those planning it for their retirement.

"Paul and I feel blessed that our work as authors, speakers and television producers of the Distant Shores Sailing Adventure TV Series, as well as other travel documentaries, has enabled us to keep earning our living while exploring the world by sailboat for almost thirty years now."

And here's how they make money. They're full-time television producers, filming when they're on the boat and editing when they're home.

Their main form of income is from license fees from TV broadcasters. They also earn money through product placement and sponsorships in the TV series and speaking engagements. They earn royalties on their books and DVDs. In the near future this revenue will likely come from YouTube.

Sheryl and Paul could also rent out their property, while living on the boat, as another revenue stream, but they choose not to, since their schedule varies too much and they have a part-time employee that works in their home office managing the administrative side of the business, book and DVD orders, etc.

They have turned their passion for sailing into a full-time business. They've honed their skills in videography and photography to create documentaries of sailing the world, and it all sounds pretty awesome to me.

Greg & Rachel Denning Discover, Share And Inspire As A World School Family

Rachel Denning had never owned a passport, until she was married with four children. While pregnant with their 4th baby, she took a trip to Mexico (back when only birth certificates were required) with her husband, Greg, and a flame was ignited for more adventure.

That trip also helped her realize she wanted her children to learn languages, experience cultures and customs, and have the world as their classroom.

So in 2007, she and Greg sold their belongings, packed up the SUV and drove with their four children - all under the age of four - through Mexico and Central America to Costa Rica, where they planned to live indefinitely.

But they couldn't stay put, and since then, they have pursued long-term family travel for over ten years, living in and traveling to more than thirty countries on five continents - and adding three more children along the way.

As a family, they have discovered that the world is too big to stay in one place. There is too much to see, to do, and to experience. Their family motto is to 'live a good story,' and much of their decisions, big and small, are measured against whether or not it will make a good story.

One of the most common questions Greg and Rachel receive about their lifestyle is, '*how do you pay for it*?'

> "That hasn't always been an easy question to answer. We didn't know the answer for many years. We asked others and tried lots of things, many of which failed, before finding our "financial groove."

The one thing they learned along their journey, meeting other travelers and expats, was that it *was* possible to live this lifestyle, *if* you wanted it bad enough. This knowledge gave them the inspiration to never give up until they found their answer.

> "There is not just one financial answer to funding long-term travel or an international lifestyle. There are as many options as there are people. Some work for a government embassy, start a business abroad, or work remotely. Others are 'digital nomads,' providing business support online, or managing their own online empires."

The Denning's funding, has morphed over the years, but they currently earn an income from Greg's mentoring and teaching of home-schooled and online students, as well as leading outdoor and international youth and family trips.

In 2017, he guided students to learn about WWII in Europe; do humanitarian work in Guatemala; backpack in Colorado; adventure camp with peers in Utah and climb to Base Camp in Nepal, not to mention being a keynote speaker at the Family Adventure Summit.

Rachel's work doesn't pay, except in ways that aren't measured in currency.

Travel planning for a family of nine is nearly a full-time job. Educating and cleaning up after her seven balls of fire, takes up the rest of her time. Whatever is left over is spent writing their memoirs.

> "Traveling with your family is not only doable, it's like a MasterCard commercial. It's priceless. And you will never regret making the decision and the effort to do it, no matter how insurmountable the obstacles may seem at times."

Erin Mcneaney Created Ongoing Revenue Building Apps

Erin McNeaney and Simon Fairbairn created ongoing revenue building apps and travel blogging.

After 12 months of world travel, Erin and her partner, Simon Fairbairn, struggled to adjust to being back in working life mode and felt suffocated by the restrictions of their office. They longed for the variation that travel had brought to each day of their round the world trip.

> "We realised life was too short to be unhappy so we decided to make a big change," Erin explains. "About six months after our return, I came across a number of digital nomads earning a living online and I thought, 'If they can do it, why can't we?'".

After coming to the conclusion that travel was something the duo could sustain through freelancing online, they booked a one way ticket to Rio de Janeiro and set about condensing their possessions into only those items they could fit in their carry-on allowance.

They initially financed their travels through Simon's freelance web design and development work while growing their now successful travel blog, Never Ending Voyage, which began to earn an income from advertising after a year.

Two years into their travels, Erin and Simon moved away from the traditional monetization streams of advertising and freelance work to create their own products.

Their main app, Trail Wallet, is a travel expense tracking app that has been downloaded by 150,000 travellers and featured by Lonely Planet, The New York Times, and The Huffington Post.

Erin credits the reach and influence of the online platform the pair had built through their blog as a contributing factor to the app's success. She says they would never have started the blog or created apps if they hadn't been nomadic. Their business is inspired by their travels.

After eight years as digital nomads, Erin and Simon's income is primarily from the app, affiliate commissions from the blog, and sales from Erin's book, *The Carry-On Traveller*, about how to pack light for any trip. These passive income sources allow them to work an average of 15 hours a week and frequently take time offline to travel.

Erin says that it's not easy running your own business, but the freedom it gives is absolutely worth it.

Model Number #2 is Selling Other People's Stuff

Many people are not fond of being in the limelight or building a business around them and some aren't actually suited for it - remember your superpowers from the assessments I hope you took, or at least looked into, from Chapter 4.

In large part, your values and desires will reveal this to you.

The great news is there are plenty of ways to build profitable businesses that don't need you to be at the forefront, doing all the work.

That's because there are plenty of other people and companies out there with great products and services you can promote, distribute and resell to build a lucrative freedom business.

In fact, this can be a highly profitable model, with very low setup cost because most of the work is being done for you in terms of the actual product. You'll end up with residual or passive revenue streams that often you to put your business on autopilot.

You can sell:

- As a distributor, such as, joining a consumer distribution network (also known as network marketing) of existing products like Nuskin.

- An affiliate for both physical and digital products or services.

- By setting up an ecommerce site to sell physical products.

Felix Page Created An eCommerce Business From Scratch

After finishing University and a Startup Accelerator program - where I mentored their team - Felix was always attracted to the idea of being his own boss, calling the shots and choosing his own work/life routine.

He stumbled across a guy on YouTube, roughly his age, who was living the digital nomad life in South East Asia and wanted to learn more. That's when he discovered Amazon Fulfillment By Amazon (FBA) as a means to start making money on the side.

"From there, one door just opened after another. I learned as much as I could and started applying it by selling products, like sunglasses to customers much like myself, using Facebook Advertising. This gave me an added advantage as I knew what was selling well on the market and the language to use to really connect with them."

This then exposed him to the idea of earning money solely from online work and decided to try and make it a full-time income.

"I started out with Amazon FBA and then, switched to dropshipping on my own website. This allowed me to experience the importance of branding, positioning and delivering the best to my customers. And evidently replace my day job."

Felix set up and started his ecommerce dropship store on Shopify in September 2016, and by December he was making NZ$20,000 a month in sales!

"I currently still run my own ecommerce store, have hired two virtual assistants to free up much of my time, and am now looking towards my next venture, which is consulting and training others who want to create their own full time income stream through eCommerce."

In this example, Felix started out with Method 1 and is going to transition into Method 2 to combine the revenue streams, and align more with giving back, versus just making money.

As he's shared his journey with his friends and through his Facebook group, he's been asked over and over to set up a training program. He listened and will deliver a solution to their needs, based on his sweet spot.

In May 2018, I too started an entirely new business in eCommerce that tapped into the fast-growing online shopping trend, combined with the dog lovers market, who spend ridiculous amounts on their fur babies each year.

I started a Shopify site, using my two gorgeous White German Shepherds as my muses - and the face of the brand. Initially I used dropshipping (selling other brand's products via my site for a markup) to test what dog products people would buy.

I then went on to source better and custom products from global suppliers - both locally and overseas, and sell them via my shop and Amazon FBA.

To challenge myself and others to do this, I ran one of my paid Freedom Labs - a live 'doing' course, to see if I could earn $3,000 in revenue in three months, starting from scratch and helping others do the same.

While that Lab made me US$10,000 in revenue in the five days it was open for registration, it turns out the three month timeline was ambitious!

In less than a few weeks I had my shop up and making sales, but the entire process was far more challenging than I realised and took upfront investment, a lot of learning and patience to get going.

However I made my $3K in 3 months on Amazon once my first product was up which was a fantastic result!

My aim is to grow this, or another eCommerce business to bring in 4-5 figures in passive revenue per month and more financial and lifestyle freedom.

Richard Patey Found Freedom Selling Online Businesses And Affiliates

Richard quit his job back at the end of 2009 with the desire to make a living from his laptop. He set up a company just so he could be called a director, whilst trying to make a living playing online poker.

That career choice didn't go well for him and he had to figure out how to make money online through business instead.

He started selling marketing services, where he would charge a client a small amount for a project, which would fund his learning and would then be confident charging much more the next time.

Richard ended up building a small SEO agency, which he sold back in 2013, which is when I met him in Vegas. I was there promoting the recent publication of my first book.

Richard had also just self-published his own book titled, '*Coffee Shop Entrepreneurs,*' about how he built up his remote income and was looking to move away from services to products.

His next business was a service offering selling pre-packaged and fixed priced marketing services to the ski industry.

Next, Richard set up a new domain, *Funnel Engine,* which offered sub $1,000 'done for you' funnel packages to other online entrepreneurs, which was generating over $5,000 per month and would also land high ticket clients paying as much as $25K for a custom sales funnel.

However, it wasn't until he sold a small ecommerce business last year that he realised he had the talent and ability to create online assets that other people valued. He could achieve a viable career and financial freedom by building up and selling online assets.

He has since transitioned his ski and funnel sites into authority content sites, with the latter monetised through software affiliate commissions. By writing about and promoting software that solves people's problems you can get paid up to 40% recurring commissions as long as they remain a customer.

Richard now makes more than his previous job through his portfolio of online sites and substantially more when he sells a web property. He hosts the Freedom Flipping Podcast, where he talks about his approach and interviews others doing the same.

Natalie Cutler-Welsh Used The Power Of Her Network To Connect The Dots

My former mastermind client and now friend, Natalie Cutler-Welsh is an Author, Speaker, Podcaster and a big advocate for residual income and 'selling other people's stuff'.

After running her business Go to Girl Ltd for 6 years, that was primarily service based, she has switched her business model up considerably and to great effect when she dived into the world of multi-level marketing.

> "My business is based around connecting people, so if someone has a problem or wants a particular product or service, I can recommend someone or a program that I genuinely think is awesome.
>
> Often I will be an affiliate or referrer for that product or service and receive a commission if a person buys via my URL link or promo code. If someone says, gosh I'm really struggling with XYZ or do you know someone who (insert skill). I can say, yes I do and let me introduce you.
>
> Then a few years ago one of my high level clients recommended doTerra essential oils to me and I fell in love with them. She happened to be number #1 representative for sales in doTerra essential oils in New Zealand.
>
> I signed up to join them as their products had made a huge impact on my health and I was already recommending them to friends and clients.

What started for me as yet another way for me to fulfil my obsession with helping my community, soon developed into a smart and strategic way for me to earn residual income while still being able to do what I love - empower, connect and mentor people."

In just 2.5 years as a Wellness Advocate for doTerra she's attracted and empowered an amazing team of leaders (many of whom were previous clients who added doTerra to their business) and is one of just 10 Founders of DoTerra in New Zealand having reached the rank of Diamond, earning NZ$12k-$15k per month.

For Natalie, it's not just about the money but what the money allows her to do, be and have in your life. She calls it the 'exponential potential for income and impact'.

"I now have over 1800 customers who are moving towards better wellness because of the oils, but I didn't have to serve them all myself! It's an amazing business model and provides residual income that allows me to be flexible and location independent.

In addition to that, as a Diamond I now have income to be able to support various projects and charities in my local community and country to a much greater capacity.

By selling 'other people's stuff' you can extend the impact that you can have on other's lives (help people to do what they WANT) but you don't necessarily need to be the one to create and deliver it. You get to stay in your own zone of genius."

Which Revenue Stream(S) Are Best Suited To You?

In addition to understanding which methods will suit you best, you also want to decide on how you will continue to earn and generate revenue.

Again there are two ways to do this - active and residual.

Some may argue there are three, which are, active, residual and passive. The thing is I don't believe there is any truly passive income - as in set it and forget it and never work again.

The closest to this would be if you put your earnings or savings into a managed investment fund, here you're less likely to have to do much work at all to make a profit over time.

However, you do have to do 'some' work upfront in choosing the best investment fund, and doing your due diligence.

Then you will need to check in with your broker, at least annually, to check on the performance of your stock. Mind you, that's about as hands off as you can get.

The same *can* apply to real estate. I own several properties in New Zealand Portugal. I invested in those as my business grew.

Two are purely investment and I rent them via AirBnB or local platforms like TradeMe in New Zealand. Another is rented all year round, and I block out 1-2 months a year for me to stay there and use my car I store there and my surfboard!

These properties provide a great, recurring four-figure monthly residual revenue, and I invest any profits back into more property when possible.

There is some work involved in getting new tenants signed up, and when people move in and out or do short term stays, as well as costs like utilities, rates, insurance and maintenance. But all of this is offset by the profit made, and of the course the capital gain on my investments.

To make this truly passive, I hire students to become my Airbnb guest manager and cleaner in New Zealand, letting guests in when I'm not there and changing over the room, and in Portugal I have Maria, a former boutique hotel employee, to do the same.

It's brilliant and a great way to outsource those things you don't have time, or want to spend time doing yourself. They take care of almost all the details and of course my guests.

1. Active - More Work, More Money

Active income typically comes from a service-based approach, such as, running a program, coaching, consulting, teaching or membership-based work and it's active because you are committing time to this on a weekly basis and actively working on it - those described in Method 1.

For example, if you choose to run a membership site you need to initially be in there doing the work, turning up to live coaching calls or trainings and managing members' expectations.

If this will be an on-going membership community, it would really suit a Wealth Dynamics Support or Trader profile (see Chapter 4 for more details on how to take the test). If on the other hand, you are a Star or Creator profile, shorter and more time-limited groups would typically get you more into flow. It means you're in flow.

For a Mechanic, like Sylvia van de Logt, who runs 40plusstyle.com and 40plusentrepreneur.com, when she launched her membership club in early 2017, she quickly realised that she was not in flow when dealing with customer management.

Her launch had proven extremely popular with her community and before she knew it, she had 160+ members and a great new recurring revenue stream.

After attending my retreat and understanding her Entrepreneurial Superpower Profile, she understood that the way it was currently set up, made her feel too tied to having to maintain and launch new content.

Instead she switched to bringing in an expert to help with trainings and present, so that it didn't all fall on her shoulders. This person now also supports the community and creates regular videos.

2. Residual - Recurring Revenue, Less Work

This is the best type of revenue for your business, especially if you want more freedom and location independence.

It means you do the work upfront, and you do it well. But after the initial setup, launch and work you, then put systems in place and automate as much as possible.

Naturally there will be some ongoing marketing and maintenance, but the rest can be automated. I've detailed a few examples below.

Software

You can see from the examples I've shared earlier in this chapter that building apps or software that solves a problem, can be very lucrative. From my own experience in co-founding a technology company, I also know the setup costs are significantly higher and your investment over the long term will be too.

However, done right, and using a well thought out sales funnel, you can consistently get you new leads and paid users. This will lead to consistent ongoing revenue and will be much easier to grow and scale.

Dan Norris had been 'failing in entrepreneurship for 7 years,' before launching *WP Curve* in 2013 - a service that provides unlimited WordPress support and small jobs, 24/7 from $79 a month.

Eighteen months later, he had a co-founder in the U.S., a team of 38 people, 850 customers passed the AUD$ 1 million dollar mark and then sold it to GoDaddy in 2016!

Affiliates

If you don't have any offerings of your own, you can promote others through affiliate marketing. You just need an audience or a list who trust you and then you need to carefully choose companies that you know, like and trust.

Once you've joined their affiliate program, you will get your own unique URL link to use to promote them, as well as swipe copy to use for emails and social media posts, plus banner ads and imagery.

Around 30% of my annual revenue is through affiliate commissions that I earn through products and tools I love, and recommend to others, like *Teachable, ConvertKit* and *ClickFunnels* - the three main systems I use to run my business.

I talk about these tools and others in emails, in blog post reviews, Facebook live videos, in my free downloadable toolkit on my website, and through jointly hosted webinars with the product and service providers themselves.

This not only covers my costs per month for using these tools, but adds thousands of dollars to my bottom line as more and more people sign up to try them out, because they trust me and my recommendations.

Sponsorship

This is another form of this sort of income and a great form of revenue, once you've built a platform. It doesn't have to be huge for sponsors to be interested either, especially if you've carved out a niche they want to get in front of.

I had great sponsors for my podcasts who bought packages that fitted their needs and in return they got access to my podcast listeners, readers of my blog and emails, as well as consumers of my social media updates.

I built a great relationship with them, typically by using and enjoying their product, or through honest reviews on my blog, and then they get a return on investment by advertising their product, by tapping into my existing community.

Sponsorships made up a big chunk of my revenue, to the tune of $100,000 in 2015-2017 alone. This revenue stream is a no brainer when you have an audience and great relationships with companies you like and use.

Putting it all together

The ideal setup is that you should have several revenue streams within your freedom business so that you're never relying on just one form of income.

Depending on your sweet spot, you may be better suited to active versus residual income. Stay true to what feels best for you and layer your revenue streams over time.

As you know, my first revenue stream was an active one when I set my Social Media Bootcamp workshops.

I then turned it into an online program and also created a digital product from there, both of which were residual.

Then, I incorporated my teachings and content into other events and retreats, so back to active income. Which then led to more products, sponsorships and affiliate marketing - residual and passive.

I know plenty of business owners that mix all of this up to suit them. Some remove all active revenue streams when they want to take time off.

Action Taking Time

You are now ready to put pen to paper and map out your business model and revenue.

By now, you should have a healthy idea of which business model suits you best, as well as several ideas for creating multiple streams of revenue.

If your current business isn't really working *for* you, what can you change to create more residual revenue and free up more time for yourself?

What You Learned In This Chapter:

- How to identify the stage you're at in your business and your next steps.

- How to find or revisit your sweet spot and entrepreneurial super-power.

- The best revenue models to fit your freedom plan and lifestyle.

In the next chapter I share my handy One Page Miracle Plan with you to do this. Let's head there now.

7

YOUR ONE PAGE "MIRACLE" BUSINESS PLAN

Having your ideal business with multiple revenue streams, sounds like a pretty grand thing to achieve doesn't it? Well it *is* completely possible so let's make it happen for you.

It is important that your business doesn't *happen to you,* instead, you design it, by choice. To do that you need to work backwards from your financial freedom goals to map out the revenue targets to make this a reality.

Before we dive into this chapter, I urge you to read Chapter 6 first, particularly if you are unclear on what type of revenue streams you want to support your business.

Let's Face the Facts

Starting and growing a business ain't easy. You've heard the statistics. More than fifty percent of businesses fail in the first four years, and according to Small Biz Trends, the leading cause of small business failure is incompetence (46%) and unbalanced experience (30%).

Understanding how your business makes you money and knowing your numbers is a big part of being a competent business owner!

What blew my mind (and these are American skewed statistics bear in mind), is that fifty one percent of small business owners are 50-88 years old!

Yes, this is partly because some freelancers wouldn't be counted in these statistics, or the younger ones swanning off around the world and working from anywhere.

Also, I believe it is because many people over the past few years have been forced to find work when they've lost their job.

And because quite frankly, they finally get to recognize their dream later in life to work for themselves and do their own thing and design their lifestyle. Except it really doesn't appear to turn out that way.

What happens is, like eighty two percent of small businesses, they use their personal savings, or that of friends and family to fund their business, and soon realize they're failing.

Why?

Because statistics state only forty percent of those small businesses started are profitable.

What the heck are the other sixty percent doing?!

Well thirty percent are breaking even and thirty percent are continually losing money. Eighty two percent of businesses that fail, do so because of cash flow problems.

And that is a sad fact I want to help change. Hence why this chapter is so damn important.

If you're reading this in chronological order, then you'll be ready to craft your beautiful One Page 'Miracle' Business Plan, if you aren't I'd love you to go back and read Chapter 5 and 6 to be prepared for this one.

My aim here is to help you better understand how to make your business grow, and build at least two revenue streams to ensure that you reach your financial freedom goals.

What is my infamous One Page 'Miracle' Business Plan method and why does it work?

No surprises here, it is a business plan that fits into one page. I know, I like to keep things simple and obvious!

I've crafted this beautiful, one-page business plan template especially for you, because over the years, actually dating back to University days, I never understood why we were 'made' to write and prepare such ridiculously long proposal documents, that no-one ever read through and that I never referred to again.

Also, I never again want to create a fifty page plus business plan, like the one we started our technology company, FundRazr. I recall thinking when we finished.

> "What a waste of time this big gigantic document is that we're never going to look at again. It's going to be covered in dust and put away in a drawer never to be used."

I think lengthy proposals however, are a pointless waste of time and energy. A pithy, succinct and action focused plan however, now that's a thing of beauty!

However, I can't disguise the fact that the research and thought put into that initial FundRazr document, did actually help shape our way of thinking around our business, and help us better understand our market and competitor landscape.

Therefore, even though this is a One Page Business Plan, it does mean you come to it *after* thinking through and doodling out the nuts and bolts of your plan on the spare page provided, or in your own individual way.

You should turn up to it with some reliable facts and figures about your business to date, for examples number of sales, customers, your website visitors, your email list, metrics from Google Analytics around where your visitors are coming from and what the heck they're doing once they find you.

In a perfect world, you'd also know these numbers like the back of your hand and check them weekly, if not more often.

Even better, you'd have someone on your team provide a report of the top and most important numbers and trends.

But I know that's not the reality for most entrepreneurs I speak too!

Then from there, you can nut out what's going to make this your best year ever and take your business to the next level.

By the way this should be fun. Not laborious. This is you getting to make more of your perfect days a reality by having a real plan in place to achieve them, over time.

That's why I've created this One Page Miracle Business Plan, that I've crafted lovingly over the years after incorporating the best bits and pieces of other tools, templates and plans I've seen and used, until I found something I was personally happy with.

In a nutshell…

- Set no more than three smart goals.

- Set your objectives to take action on those goals.

- Figure out your expenses and get clear on your monthly spend.

- Understand your revenue streams to support your annual income.

- Tell yourself why you're worth it and why this business plan is going to become to reality.

Grab your free downloadable template in my companion video series at thefreedomplan.co/start.

Using The One Page Business Plan (An Example In Action)

Start by filling out your One Page Business Plan template from the top of the page and use the blank page I've given you to doodle on and flesh out your revenue ideas and expense figures etc, before putting the final answers into the lovely template.

Next step, fill it out to the best of your ability and then print it out and post it on a wall close to your laptop where you can see every day. Print it out to a small size. Take it with you on the road. Put it in your wallet, your handbag. Put it on your phone. Make it a screensaver. It will keep you focused and on track. Trust me.

You should be revisiting your plan every month, or at least every quarter and update it as you meet or change your goals based on your progress and success. This is not going to be covered in dust. This is not getting put away in a drawer. This is a living, breathing document that you can update regularly.

Here's how to get your One Page Biz Plan done today.

Step 1: State Your Business Name

It actually starts with typing in your business name - this part is easy.

Step 2: State your Mission

Your mission is the fundamental reason you're in business, and *why* you do what you do and for who. It is the mission that you are about to go on for the rest of your life. An easy way to think through it is to answer the following statement:

I help [target] to [transformation you propose] through [your key activities].

For me, my mission is this.

> I help busy entrepreneurs achieve more personal daily freedom through life-changing habits, hacks, strategies and educational experiences.

> In 5 years from now, I would love to have helped 100,000 + people achieve more personal daily freedom, live a life they love, and have the time, money and freedom to do that every single day.

That juices me, that makes me jump out of bed every day and is the reason why I do what I do, and also, why I live by example so you can go through something like the Freedom Plan and come out the other end living life on your own terms. That is my mission in life. Your mission can be short and sweet, one line is all you need. The second part of mine is to add more context and I use it in my Operations Manual too. The second part of mine is to add more context and I use it in my Operations Manual too.

Step 3: Set Up Your Goals

Once you've got your mission sorted, then it's time to set up your BHAGS. Yep, I'm talking about your *big hairy audacious goals*. I suggest no more than three, but in my template there is room for up to five.

Less is more when it comes to goals. The more focused you are, the more likely you are to achieve them.

While I love dreaming big, there's only so much we can achieve in a year. In fact, we humans are renowned for overestimating what we can achieve in a year, but underestimating what we can achieve in five.

Therefore, factor in 'life happening.' Challenge yourself but don't make your goal so audacious you already think you can't make it happen.

You want to make your goals SMART. You've probably heard this before... but do you actually DO this when you're formulating them?

A smart goal has the following attributes.

Specific: No waffling here. You have to state succinctly and clearly what your goal is.

Measurable: You have to have a metric in there to benchmark your progress against, like a quantity or outcome you are working towards - $10,000 per month or 30% increase on last year's revenue.

Achievable: If you write down that you want to have a million dollar business in a year's time, but you have absolutely zero right now and no idea of how you're going to get that, you're probably not going to make that goal.

Realistic: If you want to become an Olympic rower in the next year, it's fairly unlikely, even if you're quite a sporty person, but you've never trained in Olympic rowing, I mean this takes a lifetime for some people to train in. So make it a stretch goal, make it challenging, but don't make it so difficult to achieve, that it becomes impossible.

Time-bound: If you don't set a date for this stuff, it will not happen. Lock it in. If you are seriously motivated, then you will move mountains to hit that date.

Let me share an example of Audie Cashion, Certified ONE Thing Trainer, Chairman and Founder of the World Peace Organization and Freedom Plan Alumni member, who loves the One Page Biz Plan. In his exact words...

"As a start-up entrepreneur of a purpose-driving non-profit organization, the World Peace Center, everything had to be tweaked multiple times not just every year, but every few weeks.

The One-page business plan was simple to create and kept me from getting stuck in a ditch and helped me move forward.

The simplicity of a one page document (I learned later) is it's remembered as a picture versus a long multi-page text document, which is not easily remembered due to how our minds recall information.

Also, when working with other team members along the way, simplicity helps with clarity and thus execution of the plan. It's easy to get buy in, when the purpose, goals and metrics for accountability are so clear.

In addition, most multi-page documents are created and never reviewed again. With my one page document it was easy to hang on the wall and refer to it daily to keep me on track.

Since I originally crafted my first The Freedom Plan business plan document, I have tweaked, re-written and re-formatted it about twenty or more times to suit my style. Yet, it still boils down to a one page document.

As Tony Robbins says, "complexity is the enemy of execution," so a one page business plan is exactly what a virtual entrepreneur needs to knock it out of the park for multiple reasons."

Let me share another example of a client I worked with on a VIP Day in San Diego. Nancy stands out as an example of someone who'd never created a business plan before, or stuck to her goals.

Using my template she figured out her offerings, her revenue streams and her path to profitability in two hours with me.

Now, Nancy like many well intentioned people I meet said, straight up, "I'd like to make six figures," and she put a date to it, which she didn't really believe in or think that she could hit. So I challenged her to change it into something that did feel doable. Here was the end result…

Grow my business by 15% on last year's result to achieve a monthly revenue of $9,000 per month by October 1, by prioritizing the three areas that bring in the most revenue.

You can see there's a date in here, there's a specific measurable $9,000 times twelve months, that's a $108,000. So there are your six figures.

The aim is to have her achieve that by October 1st by prioritizing her three revenue streams and automating them to the extent that she can time off her business for big chunks of the year.

See How Much More SMART This Goal Is?

Now, I ask you to write your own. I would suggest three goals maximum. Even though there is room for five. The more goals you set, the more objectives you're going to need to support them and the more work you're going to be doing to make this happen.

That's when things become overwhelming and your best laid plans fall apart. Whereas focusing in on just one to three goals is going to be that much easier for you to achieve what you want

For Example Your Goal Might Be:

Hire one virtual assistant and one copywriter by June 30th via Upwork.

Here's an example from my client, Jo Bendle.

Back in 2014, Jo was transitioning from a Virtual Assistant business into Productivity coaching and wanted to get really clear about her three signature offerings, get two trial VIP clients on board and launch her new look website, after doing her ideal customer avatar.

She wanted to start a business blog before the website went live so she had some content up there and wanted to introduce an extra revenue stream into her business within the next six months.

Her personal goal was to be able to work from a different country for four to six weeks within the next twelve month period.

So what did Jo achieve?

Three years later, Jo now has a thriving business as a Productivity Coach over at jobendle.com and has transitioned away from working with 1-1 clients to helping 100's of women with her group programs.

She introduced what is now her signature membership community focusing on helping women in business get more done, in less time.

She used the One Page Biz plan to focus on consistently building and growing her business.

Jo came to my Bali Freedom Mastermind Retreat in 2015, which was the start of her being 100% location independent.

She's now been running her business and traveling the world for the past three years, while earning four to five figures per month consistently - that's a productive result.

Step 4: Match Your Objectives To Meet Your Goals

A goal isn't going to happen by itself now is it? Therefore, you want to break your goals down into smaller chunks by supporting them with strategic, manageable objectives, preferably that you can do daily, but at least weekly or monthly.

Simply put, *your objectives are actions you're going to take to reach your goals* and the strategies that you are going to put in place to achieve them.

Now, back to Nancy. Her first objective to meet that goal might be spend $500 a month on targeted advertising on Google and Facebook to gain 300 new email leads per month and convert 10% of those leads into whatever package she was trying to convert them into.

Objective 2 for that goal would be to.

- Do two podcast interviews a month on shows within her niche that have a listenership of over 50,000 listeners a month.

- Write two guest posts per month on major sites in her niche.

- Land a major piece of media each month to drive 200 new leads to her list and convert 10% into paying customers. Now, you can see between these objectives, that's about 500 new people per month, which is a decent amount of people to target and convert each month. If you can convert 10% of those people, then you've got fifty new customers!

I'm going with 10% here as that's a very good conversion rate, but also totally achievable.

With fifty new customers on board to support her end goal of $9,000 per month, that means each client is worth $180 in sales, which could be made up of one course, a few eBook sales, or a membership or software subscription.

Suddenly that $9,000 a month seems that much more achievable right?

Here's a great example of how to stay focused on your business needs from Justin Krane, a Certified Financial Planner professional over at jkrane. com. He is a money strategist for business owners.

> "I have made a conscious effort to create two businesses that have programs and services that are nearly 100% recurring revenue. Any investment that I make in my business, gets measured against the likelihood that it will result in predictable, reliable, recurring income. If it doesn't, it's simply not for me.

> The best way for business owners to plan their future is to have visibility on profits, and to know how much extra cash a business generates. Having recurring revenue makes it so much easier to work towards financial peace of mind."

Step 5: Investing In Your Business (Expenses)

For this next step, we're going to look at how much it really costs to run your business.

When I first started out, I was budgeting and skimping on a lot of stuff because I didn't have much money at all.

Compare that to the last few years, where I invested $50,000+ on my team alone. This has always increased the return on investment on my business.

But I couldn't just jump straight to that level of investment in the first year when I had next to no money. This has been a six-year work in progress.

One thing I know for sure is that you have to be willing to invest in order to grow. So please don't skimp on the things that are super important to growing your business, like great branding and design, copywriting and specialists in areas you need, such as a sales funnel expert.

The minute you can, invest in those key areas and the right people, even if it seems like a stretch, or a scary move. It will pay dividends.

Break Down Your Expenses

List out things you know you're going to be spending money on this year, like your website design or upgrade, software and tools, a designer, copywriter, assistant, accountant, SEO specialist and your own education.

Simply list out your known expenses and write them directly into my template's 'Expenses' box. If you don't have any benchmark for it, do some research online.

- How much is your mobile going to cost you a year?

- Which tools and platforms will you use to run your business from? This could include an email platform, CRM, calendar management, webinar platform, sales funnel tool.

- How much does it cost to hire a search engine optimization consultant?

- Which hosting website company will you use? For example Hostgator starts from under $5 per month and WPEngine that I use are a lot more.

- Do you need regular design work done for your blog, website or social media?

- Do you need to hire a copywriter for one project and have a part -time virtual assistant? Are your team costs project based or on a monthly retainer?

When I first started my business, I'd track all expenses and income manually in a spreadsheet. My life changed the minute I switched over to XERO, beautifully simple accounting software, for tracking my full financials and reconciling all bank feeds, PayPal and Stripe automatically.

I had a completely accurate Profit and Loss report on where I was spending my money and how much I was really making.

Hiring an accountant also made a huge difference for tax savings and understanding my full financials and options. It's a substantial investment each month but they deal with my personal and business taxes and save me money each year.

This allows me to set a proper budget for my Business Plan each year and put in real numbers to benchmark off.

But when I started out, I'd 'guesstimate' and do my research online to get approximate costs for tools, services and software I might need.

Then I'd double it! Your expenses will always be higher than you budget for.

You can also ask other people what they're paying and then list those out, add them up and pop your total expenses in that box. Simple, right?

Step 6: Break Down Your Revenue Streams

This is the fun part. Just to give you an example, I have had up to nine revenue streams in my business, which included...

- Digital products (ebooks)

- Online courses

- Membership communities

- 1-1 Coaching, group coaching

- Paid speaking

- Published books

- Events and retreats I hold

- Affiliate commissions and;

- Sponsors for my podcast and my blog.

These unfolded year by year as I scaled my business. In 2017 I actively reduced them so that I'm focusing on just the highest leverage revenue activities - and ones that don't require as much of me.

Now, it's time for you to work out what it is you can offer, or expand upon in your current offerings in order to increase your revenue streams and overall revenue.

Take my template and list out those revenue streams and be specific.

For example, if you're a fitness instructor, you might want to produce an ebook that sells for $50 dollars. Your aim is to sell twenty copies a month through select marketing and social media. You can earn $12,000 a year just from that.

Fitness eBook: $50 x 20 x 12 = $12,000.

You might want to start an online bootcamp as well, made up of several learning modules, where you show them exercises via video and through workout guides.

Now, you look at your competition, work out your current hourly rate you charge clients, and estimate how many hours it will take to produce the course, and decide to charge $397 for it.

If you have ten paying customers a month and are repeatedly getting ten in a month from your sales funnel, that's going to give you about $39,700 per year!

You might want to do group fitness coaching online too. So people can buy the course, but then upgrade to get access to you for an extra $2,000 per quarter.

You could feasibly enroll eight people in your group coaching, you might cap it at this to give truly great service, so you have added.

Group coaching: $2,000 x 8 x 4 = $64,000 per year.

Your total revenue for the year is now $115,700 minus your expenses.

In the example above, I hope you can see how you can layer in offerings that allow your potential clients to go from strength to strength, and build up their investment with you, as you build trust and add value.

I would suggest you have between two to four revenue streams in your business. If one to two of those are passive or residual, that means if something happens to you and you can't work, or you wish to go on an extended vacation, you will still be making money, and be able to cover your expenses and team too.

As you use my One Page Biz Plan template, you'll start to see which of your *current* revenue streams are costing you way too much in terms of your time and not producing the revenue you need.

By detailing your streams out, you can quickly see which of these are the highest leverage activities that you should be focusing on.

Then ask yourself, is the work you're going to be doing to create these revenue streams, going to support your revenue goal for the year?

If no, don't worry. That's actually normal.

Step 7: Future Revenue Streams

Go back and look at your revenue streams and take a good hard look at the real numbers. You might find your saying to yourself:

- "Huh! Why am I doing that one-on-one coaching, when I could be doing group coaching that pays me a lot more for less work?"

- "Why am I selling that book, when I could be selling this program that is far more profitable and valuable?"

- "Why am I running that event, when I could be doing this thing instead?"

Ask yourself:

- How can I increase my prices?

- How can I gain more clients?

- How can I take on new revenue streams?

- What do I need to let go of in order to make more money to live this freedom lifestyle?

- Which revenue streams are not serving me that I can drop?

Keep asking yourself these questions every month when you review your plan, and at the same time brainstorm ways to bring in more revenue that aren't on your agenda right now.

That's it. Once a month book a date with yourself and your One Page Biz Plan and look at what's working well and what's not. Is there any opportunity that you're missing?

You can brainstorm by yourself, with peers, mentors, your mastermind or with your team.

Step 8: State Your Worth

This is one of my favourite parts of the One Page Biz Plan template. It's the *'Because I'm worth it'* section. I'm talking about listing out your credentials to remind yourself of why you are more than enough to run this business, and why you're fully capable of succeeding.

I don't care if your credentials include a life-saving certificate that you got when you were twelve years old, a volunteer certificate, any awards you have - even from school - it still counts and is important.

List any University degree(s) you have, professional qualifications, training you've undertaken - whatever it is that you've got, anything you've done that you're proud of, put it in my template under credentials.

This is going to be the place you come to first on those days of doubt, when you think, 'Who am I to try and pull this off?' Or when you're looking back at your mission and you think, 'Who am I to accomplish this? Who am I to think that I can pull this off and make this business plan come true?'

Now, when you read over this section of your plan you will think, 'Actually who am I NOT to pull this off. I'm awesome. Here's proof.

All of your amazing combined experiences and knowledge during your entire life are worth so much more than you could ever imagine. So list them out.

Step 9: Personal Growth Goals

Finally, you finish off with some personal growth goals that you have in mind for the next twelve months, because as your business grows, it's important you grow too and up level or upskill, wherever necessary, to be able to scale and cope with your success.

This may be a course you want to do, it may be a retreat or an event, or it may be hiring a personal coach, getting a mentor or joining a mastermind.

Write in this last section a couple of things that you'd love to do to increase your skills or knowledge, that you want to invest in this year and see if you can account for it with the increasing revenue you are now going to make happen.

Action Taking Time

It's time to create and polish your One Page Biz Plan. In my companion video series I've provided a free template for you to download at thefreedomplan.co/start

It is easy to fill in on Adobe Reader. You simply open it up, fill it in and save it.

I then recommend saving it as a picture to your desktop, laptop screen saver and printing it out in physical form to take with you.

There are even instructions on how to use it, plus that wonderful spare page for doodling and figuring out the details to put into your One Page Biz Plan to create your dream lifestyle business.

What You Learned In This Chapter:

- Why too many entrepreneurs fail and how you can avoid being a statistic.

- The importance of knowing your numbers to achieve financial freedom.

- How to use the One Page 'Miracle' Plan to map out your business success.

- How to set SMART Goals and actually achieve them.

8

BUILDING A LUCRATIVE SALES FUNNEL AND AUTOMATING YOUR BUSINESS

Have you ever been to an IKEA store? If you haven't you're missing out on one heck of an experience.

This Swedish founded international success story is the perfect example of an amazing sales funnel in action.

Their strong brand identity is through the Swedish flag colors of dark blue and bright yellow. So signs pointing to IKEA, while you're driving, or in magazines and online really stand out.

This continues on in their shopping bags and designer stores.

From the minute you walk into one of their huge stores, they basically have you in their grip. They've no doubt spent millions of dollars understanding the psychology behind shopping, buyer behaviour patterns and decision making.

You are taken through the showroom and displays of all their home furnishings and accessories first, where you can see everything superbly displayed, as if it's already in your home.

It's not dissimilar to the principles behind the perfect day exercise. Visualize your perfect home, set up thanks to IKEA, sparking your imagination with what's possible through their gorgeous displays.

Of course, right next door, are the individual products that you can mark down on their paper form or through their smartphone app so you can start ordering immediately.

By the time you get to the checkout counter, you'll have everything you're about to buy marked out for you and either delivered or ready for collection.

As you make your way through the store, it's like they know what you're going to do and are ready to serve your every need. I experienced this in Portugal when shopping for useful items for the house I bought.

I had a pretty specific list of what I needed, but knew that I would come out with more, even if I was really focused and they knew it too.

As my small bag I'd taken to fill up with, 'just the things I needed,' got too full because I'd added in some extras, there was a bigger bag for me to use, conveniently on display around the corner.

When that bag got full too and I found the load too heavy, a line of shopping trolleys appeared around the next corner, just in time.

This was clearly very well planned out, after years of testing what customers do when they shop in IKEA, and giving customers what they need, when they need it on their journey.

To top it off, like any smart retailer, associated products are grouped next to each other as you'd naturally want a crockery set, when you're also shopping for kitchen knives, wine glasses and chopping boards. Those ones are more obvious.

But they go the extra mile putting food storage solutions, kitchen decorations and virtually every conceivable item you, 'might,' but probably don't need in your kitchen, right in front of you so you can't resist.

Why am I telling you this? Because that, my friend, is a brilliant example of a well honed sales funnel in action! Which includes...

- Clear branding

- Great navigation

- Excellent product display

- Bundled offers

- Upselling

These are the exact same things that apply to your online business.

A great brand, an easy to navigate website, clear calls to action, products that are easy to find, along with associated products you 'must have.' Adding all of these into the cart so that when you get there it's easy to buy and have them shipped.

So What Is A Sales Funnel And Why Must You Have One?

The sales funnel is this wonderful tool that when used right, allows you to create multiple points of purchase and as a result multiple streams of revenue for your lovely online business.

It takes visitors to your website, Facebook page or landing page, on a journey and turns them into subscribers and customers as they move through your personalized sales funnel.

It's the most overlooked, yet most critical component of any successful business, and that's what I'm here to help you nail it - or at least put a basic one in place to get started on cultivating consistent and repeat business and revenue.

In a simplistic overview, this is what a sales funnel looks like.

The Top Part Is Your Freebie Offering

This can be an ebook, manifesto, video series or something they can download and opt-in to get that's very valuable, well done and shows off your expertise in a way that helps your visitor and speaks right to the heart of their problem.

The funnel is the series of logical sequences that you create to take a person on their own journey, that ensures they buy your products and services that most meet their needs, and allow you to easily grow your business.

This is also the main point at which you want to have those who are not your ideal customers actually leaving the funnel - so unsubscribing from your email list and opting out of your autoresponder series, because you don't want people on your list that aren't wanting to purchase from you.

Those that reach the bottom of the funnel, are your true red carpet clients, who've been through the journey, who have read all your emails, come to your webinars or live events, bought lower priced products from you and are now ready for the big time - your big ticket items.

That might be an online program priced at $2,000, a high end consulting, a coaching package costing $10,000 or a year long retainer to your website security services.

This is where the magic happens, because your sales funnel has worked to build trust with them over time, and now you're dealing with the right people who value your time, expertise and offerings and are prepared to invest heavily in you.

That's the beauty of a well crafted sales funnel.

The Proven Method for Building a Sales Funnel

I can't really emphasize how important this is to your business - it is critical. So much so that I've studied this in detail, emulated from the best of the best, tested, experiment, optimized and I even wrote a digital book on it.

You can start small and build out as you go. The point is that this tool will exponentially grow your business when you get it right.

Start today, and build it out bit by bit. The other great thing about a sales funnel is it forces you to evaluate your business offerings and look for all the golden opportunities.

In chapter 8 you designed your ideal One Page 'Miracle' Business Plan and fleshed out your revenue streams in Chapter 7.

Now, you have to put them into action, but building them into the sales funnel to make it a reality.

I'm assuming that right now, depending on the level of business you're at, that your sales funnel may look a little bit like this.

- You might have a call to action or a freebie opt-in on your site or blog, you probably have a few autoresponders that point towards your existing content.

- Once they've opted in, you've probably set up a few emails like a welcome email and some other valuable emails that sort of point them towards blog post etc.

- You have a few autoresponders that point them to products or services that you have, but these often come five to eight emails down the line, and are a very soft sell.

- Once customers buy from you, you don't actually have a way for them to buy further from you and you hadn't thought to promote anything else, there might not even be an option to have an upsell.

- Maybe at this point you don't have any other products, but if you do this is probably a crucial piece that you're missing.

If you're nodding your head or thinking some of this applies to you, then let's break down the steps you do need to take to start today!

The Sales Funnel in Action

The first step to building your sales funnel is to understand your customer's decision-making process, which is often referred to as the customer journey.

To do this, you have to put yourself in your customer's shoes as they first become aware of a "problem" that needs to be solved.

Then, consider each stage of the decision-making journey they go through.

You wouldn't go online to buy a treadmill and buy the first one you see - unless you're a complete impulse buyer and have a few thousand dollars to spare.

Most of us would go through a number of logical steps that help us make an the best decision for our needs.

That's what a sales funnel is - the key stages of decision-making in a customer's journey to buy from you.

Traditionally sales funnels have had four stages of:

1. Attraction

2. Interest

3. Desire

4. Action

However these funnels have often treated customers like cattle being herded to one final destination, with no thought for the individual.

Savvy online marketers and entrepreneurs use conversion funnels instead which places more emphasis on your customer's behaviour, nurturing and retention at each of their their journey.

In my mind, there's nothing better than an example in action, so I'm going to show you one of my previous sales funnels, and then the new one we designed when I re-launched my Suitcase Entrepreneur brand and website in December 2016 that was a huge success.

I'd also like you to note that this sales funnel has been a work in progress from the get go. Every single year I've grown my business, it has been as a result of better understanding my audience, my ideal customers and then making a tweak or optimization in my existing sales funnel to improve it.

I continue to update and change my sales funnel as my audience changes and as my business pivots too. You should too.

The 'Starting Out' Sales Funnel

When I discovered what a sales funnel truly was, after reading several blog posts and guides on it, back in 2012, I started out with my Freedom Starter Kit.

This was essentially a bundle of products - my *Social Media Workout Book for Entrepreneurs* (that you may remember from Chapter 5), my *Ultimate Toolkit to Run Your Business from Anywhere* PDF and a short ten minute audio on the *Four Key Things it Takes to be Free*, all in zip file.

That zip file was hosted in Dropbox and I shared the public link to it in the welcome email you got once you'd opted in. Simple and it worked really well.

Once people actually opted in, whether through a Facebook advert, my blog, a guest post, a guest interview or any social media link I shared, they would automatically receive a set of eight autoresponders from me, spaced out over three weeks.

These emails were quite meaty and really valuable, and took them through my six steps to building a profitable online business. Throughout that email series I introduced them to my products with an understated: If you'd like to learn more about this topic, you might want to checkout my *BYOB Build Your Online Business Guide*.

Typically what happens, is after reading some of my blog posts, watching my videos and receiving a few of my emails, they would actually go and buy one of my guides, depending on what price point they want to start at ($19-57) and what they are interested in.

Then from there the whole aim of the sales funnel is to drive them to consider joining the Freedom Plan program or even to come to a workshop or retreat - a much higher price ticket item they were willing to invest in, as I'd consistently built trust over time.

- With digital guides, anyone can buy them at any time and they are unlimited.

- With the Freedom Plan, while technically there are no limits, the intake is more exclusive when run live each year to keep the group coaching calls intimate.

- For my retreats I typically capped them at no more than ten to twelve attendees.

Now, you may be wondering how long it was between website visitor, to option to sale. I know of many people who would 'linger' in my community for six months or more before purchasing anything from me. Others who'd never heard of me, would come across my work and sign up for a retreat.

They were typically looking for the very solution I offered, and ready to commit.

Most people, however, are typically willing to invest a smaller amount in you to 'test you out' first. This is where I see so many entrepreneurs miss out.

When someone first opts in to your list, and therefore, the start of your sales funnel, you simply HAVE to place an offer in front of them right away. Nothing too big, something of high value but under $20 has been proven to work best. A high value email series, video training, masterclass or a really useful checklist etc.

Years ago you'd never hear me speak like this, in fact, I felt that was way too sales-ey and felt icky. But you simply do not want a bunch of people on your email list who are never prepared to buy from you, and are also known as 'tire kickers.'

The best way to test this out, is immediately. I see too many people (including myself) missing the opportunity to say, "Hey, since you're here, and looking for XYZ, here's this great offer/ thing I have that might help."

They can choose to say no thanks, leave by unsubscribing or purchasing it. Each of these options means you are left with an engaged audience who will actively buy from you. Not a bunch of freeloaders who intend to consume all your free content that you spend hours putting together, with no intention of ever buying from you.

After visiting so many people's websites, if I like their content or style, I would immediately look around their site to see what they had on offer that I could buy.

Why? Because I was the right customer, in the right place, at the right time with the right pain point that person or product solved.

The New and Improved Sales Funnel

In late 2016, I did a complete makeover of my brand, my website and my systems and man did it feel good!

Every two years or so, I recommend upgrading and refreshing your branding and making sure it's aligned with who you are, where your business is and what values you want people to associate you with.

This time we went for fun, modern and adventurous for the brand. The site got stripped back from one hundred pages and over nine hundred blog posts, to around nine pages in total.

The site speed went through the roof, and once all the broken links were fixed and a whole lot of messy code from previous website redesigns cleaned up, traffic grew like crazy again and the SEO kicked in big time.

With that rebrand, meant a makeover for my existing free options, templates and products. It was a big piece of work spanning around six weeks and I was impressed at what we achieved.

In addition, I worked with Sasha Peakall, a Freedom Plan Alumni member who's become a sales funnel whizz. Together we transformed what I had, taking the best bits and reinventing the rest. I continue to improve it on a regular basis.

The 'Are you cut out to be a freedom entrepreneur' quiz, made a comeback from being buried somewhere on my old site, to being front and centre as one of our revolving home page opt-ins.

From there, anyone who takes the quiz, instantly gets their individual result and a list of useful resources and content on my blog that will help them.

If they opt-in they will get a beautiful PDF summary of their results telling them what stage they're at in their business and what they can focus on to improve.

In addition, we provide them with a few key resources from my blog that will help them and the best products suited to *them*. This leads to regular daily sales.

You want to put your best work out front, so people know what to expect of you, and the quality you'll deliver if they purchase further offerings from you.

Getting Granular With Your Audience

The other brilliant thing about the quiz is it puts my audience for that website into one of four categories:

1. Just starting out or wanting to quit their 9-5.

2. Freelancing or doing a side hustle and wanting to take it full time

3. In business already, but working too hard and wanting to systemize

4. Doing well in business and now wanting to have more freedom while scaling.

Each different avatar has been carefully and lovingly crafted after years of surveying my audience to understand where they're at.

Once they get their quiz results and PDF, they get a series of autoresponder emails, between six to eight and we add to these over time and can change them up depending on how they're doing opens and clicks wise.

These emails are specifically for them and are a mix of education, advice and promoting products for where they're at in their stage of the journey.

From there, for any future announcements and products, we can be very targeted and specific in who we email, and this gets us much better results, and saves us from pissing off people who just aren't interested in what we're delivering because it doesn't resonate or apply to them.

Therefore, it's a win-win.

Right now you may be thinking to yourself, oh yes, my one measly sales funnel is too generic, not targeted enough and doesn't convert well at all. Hopefully now you know why this is!

Squeezing Your Funnel Further

The thing is, once I started using <u>ClickFunnels</u> for my landing, optin and sales pages, and saw how they structure out their funnel templates, upsells and cross-sells. I realised there's a whole new world of opportunities out there waiting for you to take advantage of them.

For too many years I had the 'one size fits all' sales funnel. It was good and it worked, but it certainly was not half as effective as it could have been.

I was treating everyone the same, and not considering where they were at in their stage of business and lifestyle. Now I have several different offerings to use and test for conversions.

Based off the results of the quiz we've analysed, we can see where most of our audience are at from a business standpoint. So we know what products we should be creating and launching to meet their needs.

This is absolute GOLD when it comes to growing and scaling your business, without you working longer and harder.

That's what the sales funnel does. It takes your audience on a journey to meet their own needs. Do the work up front to lay the foundations, then continue to tweak and optimize every month to achieve stellar results.

Starting from a simple affordable offer that helps them immensely, you will then take your customer through the funnel all the way to your 'high ticket' offer, such as a coaching package, an event, a retreat or a programme.

The point of the funnel is that people naturally get squeezed out of it or self select to leave, as they go through. This is a great thing. You don't want everyone to be your ideal client and not everyone needs what you have, or can afford it.

And by the time they've been on the journey, only the most committed and ideal clients and customers remain, and you get to serve them with your best ability!

Sales Funnel Example In Action

Derek Murphy runs creativindie.com and a couple of years ago was doing book cover designs and making over $10,000 a month. The trouble is he was stressed out and working way too hard to please clients.

> "I wanted to be focusing on passive income products so I could spend more time building new assets, rather than, always chasing new payments from new clients.
>
> So I put in place a sales funnel that included affordable DIY book design templates, midrange online courses and high-end book design and coaching.
>
> And now I have more time to write books. As a result I went from $100 a month to $5000+ a month in Kindle ebook sales and I'm getting close to $5,000 a month, mainly from the templates package."

So What Does Derek's Sales Funnel Look Like?

> "For cover design work I get leads and referrals from writing a lot of articles about book design: what kind of covers sell books, case studies and examples. I also try to be proactive about speaking at writing conferences.

I *should* do a lot more guest posts to boost traffic, but I hate asking for approval, so instead I bought up a lot of expired domains related to publishing to boost SEO.

I also talk about publishing on my main blog and then I invested in some online tools, like a free ISBN barcode generator or a free ebook conversion tool.

Since my business is pretty unique and I got in early, I rank well for "book cover design." I get a few thousand visitors a day across multiple sites and have never had to chase clients."

When it comes to passive income streams, Derek takes a different approach, because he needs to maximize his traffic and conversions across all his platforms.

He's following a tried and true method espoused by the likes of Russell Brunson at Click Funnels or Jeff Walker, which he generously shares here.

"People search for book design templates or how to design/ format a book, and either find my YouTube tutorials or my website on the first page of Google. Out of two thousand visitors a day, I get about fifty opt-ins.

Right now, my email funnel goes like this...

- Here's the free stuff, you can upgrade to a premium package, but only for the next few days.

- Value add 1

- Value add 2

- Value add 3

I share everything I know about book design, formatting and marketing, plus a bunch of links back to my site to boost traffic and establish myself as an authority.

Each email ends with a P.S. you have 3, 2, 1 more days to upgrade.

Then an email with "last chance," to get the premium package and save big, with more details about what's included and some testimonials. Then, I continue with more advanced book marketing and publishing tips.

- Value add 4

- Value add 5

- Value add 6

After that I begin an evergreen course launch series to sell my higher price course. This was the first course I created in late 2016 and made $18,000 off.

Now, it's in Evergreen mode (delivered automatically, not live) and because I know what I'm doing, I'll start investing more in lead-gen, by advertising through a sales funnel that looks like this.

- Free eBook

- Free challenge

- 1 month of free book promotion

- $47 book design package

- Free video series

- Free email series

- Free 3D book promotion graphics...

From my existing traffic, I make a couple hundred bucks a day on autopilot, however, now that I've built some passive income, I can start to scale it in a big way, something I could never do with my cover design business.

Now, let's dive into how Derek makes money through writing and publishing fiction.

"When I started publishing fiction, I built a list of 8,500 targeted readers by running book giveaways with KingSumo (a WordPress plugin for giveaways). Advertising to readers who liked those books or authors on Facebook, and offered them a free sample of my book.

After building a platform for my writing, and learning how to make my books stick on Amazon, I'm making about $5,000 a month with book sales – and I can grow that number quickly now that I'm writing full-time.

What I've learned is I need to meet potential customers where they are, not where I want them to be. For example, far more authors search for, "how to write a book" than "how to market a book," (there are more people, earlier in the process of doing something, than those who have finished it).

Then, once they've finished, they'll be looking for an agent and an editor, and probably exploring traditional publishing before they figure out they want to self-publish.

So I need resources that answer what they're actually looking for, and become a helpful guide for them in that process. When they're finally ready for book design, formatting, or marketing – they'll already know who I am."

It's a brilliant example as Derek has clearly thought through the needs of his customers, and is providing solutions for them for where they're at now. Knowing this, will lead to further revenue as they progress through his sales funnel on their journey.

I hope I have convinced you just how lucrative a well thought through sales funnel will be to your business - driving you new leads, customers and ongoing sales. Once you have one up and running, the sky is truly the limit!

The trick is to start simple and not overcomplicate it. There will be a time when your sales funnel or conversion funnel as I prefer to call it, could be complex beast of well thought out options and pathways for each stage of your customer's journey, depending on what you sell and how well you understand their intentions, desires and behaviours.

One thing is for sure, if you don't have a basic funnel in action today then you are missing out on a critical function of your sales, marketing and customer retention process. Don't let that happen. Invest in this more than anything else and it will return you dividends.

What You Learned In This Chapter:

- The importance of understanding exactly what your customers desire.

- Why your sales funnel is the most critical piece of your business.

- What it takes to build a lucrative sales funnel.

- Examples of sales funnels in action that you can apply.

STAGE 3

FREEDOM LIFESTYLE

9

HOW TO SCALE YOUR BUSINESS WITHOUT YOU

When I think back over my first year of business, it was full of hustle. I was writing posts, creating digital products, growing my social profiles, networking and every other possible task. To say it was exhausting would be an understatement.

Yes, I loved what I was doing, but it didn't feel very scaleable at the time.

What I've noticed over the years is that many of us entrepreneurs aren't quite sure how to build a business that can scale and grow at the same time.

I'd like you to entertain the thought that by removing YOU as the bottleneck in your business, could in fact, help it grow and scale beyond your wildest dreams.

Additionally, you'll regain the time you've been craving to do whatever the heck you want to be doing, free from guilt of not being 'busy' for the sake of it.

Most entrepreneurs I talk to don't actually contemplate that firing themselves as the CEO of their own business, could actually help them to be more successful.

Why Is That?

I'd like to reveal to you something commonly known as the SUPERHERO syndrome. That is when you do EVERYTHING yourself because you...

1. Believe you're the best and only person to do it.

2. Don't have anyone else to delegate overwhelming tasks.

3. Are a perfectionist (aka procrastinator) and won't release anything until it's amazing.

Well it doesn't have to be that way. I'm going to share with you **the step by step process** to get out of your own way, reclaim your most precious asset - TIME - and generate more revenue as a result.

Why is this so important?

Well, you deserve to have a business that gives you more freedom. Yet, often we're so caught up in our day-to-day lives that we can't even begin to imagine what that would look like.

Imagine taking the afternoon off or bringing your weekend forward into the middle of the week to go cycling, relax in a park, read a book by the water or get away for a two day hike, to check-into a fancy hotel or spend quality time with your partner or family?

Personally, freedom is my highest value in life, it means I can do what I want, when I want, with who I want. It means I have the power of choice.

I can choose to work on my business or go on an adventure.

Yet, I meet far too many people everyday who seem completely limited in their choices and trapped in a cycle. This is because they've not worked out their definition of freedom or put any systems or measures in place to actually achieve it.

So let's put a stop to that shall we?

Do You Own A Business Or A Job?

If you're at the helm of your own business, acting like a superhero, with no extra help, then you currently own a job.

That's not what you want, trust me. You want to own a business system and be a true business owner.

I encountered this for myself several times over in the first few years of business when everything depended on me; as you may remember reading in Chapter 1.

But in early 2017, I realised I'd fallen into the trap of running a successful business that was all based around my brand, which was me.

So when I was ready for a business sabbatical, essentially firing myself, I had a harder time than I thought, despite my systems, great small team and sales funnels I'd already put in place.

I thought the business might slow down or decline, as I'd removed several revenue streams; like group coaching, live launches, workshops and retreats.

But there was one important ingredient that just couldn't be outsourced.... and that was ME.

I realised that things I wanted to hand over, say to an interim CEO, weren't easy to delegate, such as...

- Seven years worth of goodwill built up through endless content, emails, videos, and podcasts.

- My relationship with my community who have all been a part of my journey and growth.

- Relationships with key companies and people for sponsorships and partnerships.

- An intimate knowledge of what's worked and what hasn't in my business to date, and how to capitalize on the opportunities ahead of us.

My advice to you right NOW, is to build a BUSINESS that you can separate from, should you wish to in the future.

Sure put your brand and personality behind it, but have ways to earn revenue that aren't based on you being at the forefront of your business.

Take someone like Tony Robbins, the #1 Personal Transformation Guru in the world. He still does his huge live events to thousands of people, but the rest of his global team run and operate his business. He has certified coaches who can teach and run satellite events, conduct workshops, and sell his products for him.

He's scaled to a huge degree, even though it's his personal brand, but it has taken time.

Or David Finkel, after growing his business to a couple hundred thousand dollars per year, David felt like it's ability to grow had plateaued because the business relied so heavily on him working seven days a week.

Having learnt from this experience, he started from scratch with the sole purpose of building a business that was easy to scale. He then took back his time and gained more adventure in life and freedom in business. He says:

> "One of the biggest mistakes I see a business owner make early on is that they are so happy to find an opportunity that they will spread themselves thin and chase every opportunity. What happens is they become very unfocused and don't recognize the true cost of this to their business and personally.
>
> One of the things that helped us grow is by stating who are we going to say no to, so that we focus on a niche. Then,

we can actually start to understand our cost of sale, cost of marketing, our cost of fulfillment and development of products for more sales.

In our book *Scale: Seven Proven Principles to Grow Your Business and Get Your Life Back,* we talk about creating a time value matrix.

You simply sit down and write on paper.

- What things do we do that create the most value for the business?

- What are those things that you do that create the least value for the business?

With those five or six hours of time, now it becomes a choice of figuring out which are those fewer and better places, that if you were to focus on, would make a bigger difference?

Then just take a little bit of extra energy around the most important things that you do and start to systematize them. You don't have to have a perfect system just a draft of a system.

When I hire somebody I can say, "Hey Sheila, you handle these things and here is the start to the systems we have for them." Now she can take that from a structure and she has a much greater odds of being successful taking on those roles.

Don't just replace yourself with a person, but incrementally bit by bit, start to replace yourself from pieces of the business with the right person, with the sound business system and with a simple control."

Right. Let's Get Started Shall We?

Now, I warn you some of these steps may seem overly simple to you, but that's because, this isn't rocket science, it's not complicated.

But it does take discipline, time and the right guidance from someone who's been there and mastered it. That's where I come in to help you!.

Magically releasing yourself from the nitty gritty of your business won't happen overnight, but it will happen in seven days or less if you follow my plan!

Rescue Yourself

For EVERY single person I speak to they all have the same three key challenges. They don't have enough time, money or freedom.

Then you become…

- Worried about not having enough money.

- Worried about not being able to pay salaries.

- Afraid of needing to go back to your day job and admit your business failed.

- Worried you don't spend enough time with your loved ones.

- Don't have consistent recurring revenue coming in.

- Just don't have enough time,

The thing is ALL of these challenges and fears can be taken care of when you start by rescuing YOURSELF.

To do that, we need to do an exercise that will be very revealing, potentially painfully so. It's called a TIME THIEF audit and it looks like this.

1. Add up how many hours you're currently working each week.

I highly recommend using Toggl.com to tell you EXACTLY where your time is going - and it's free. It's a really neat piece of software that tracks what you're doing based on what you say is productive work vs. nonproductive - and then sends you a useful weekly report showing you exactly where you spent your time and on what.

Suddenly, you see that Gmail consumed 7 hours 52 mins of your time and that you wasted 4 hours 37 mins on Facebook, and you get a big reality check on how you're truly spending your time!

2. Then ask yourself (honestly) how many of those hours are spent on non-revenue generating tasks?

By that I mean, did creating images for your blog in the Canva app, Snapchatting your friends, and checking the newsfeed in Facebook really contribute to your bottom line?

- How many of those 7 hrs 42 mins in email were spent growing your business?

- What were you doing that didn't deserve your time and attention?

- Where is the time thief in your life?

You need to get into the mindset that any activity that is not going to lead you to make more money or serve your business is a waste of time, and time is precious.

Take this example: Gabrielle has a web design business and currently charges $75 per hour to her clients.

However, she's only spending 12 hours per week working on client projects, and 20 hours per week on operations, marketing and admin.

Now, some of these activities are for sure important in the running of her business, and even in servicing her clients, or potentially attracting new ones. That doesn't mean SHE should be doing them.

Imagine if she hired a virtual assistant for $13 per hour to take over 10 of those hours.

For $130 per week, she's freed up 10 of her own hours to use for client work worth $750 (10 x $75ph). That's almost a 7X return on investment!

Now this is only for a single week - imagine what happens when you apply this to the next 12 months of business and you start to see how immensely powerful delegating these tasks will be for you and how much easier it will be to hit your revenue goals.

Think about it. Let's say you want to make $120,000 a year, but you only want to work 5 hours a day and take 8 weeks off a year plus every weekend off.

Doing the math $120,000, 200 days, five hours a day - you'd need to earn $120 per hour.

So now you know that for the five hours you're working per day, you need to be focused on tasks that make you $120 per hour or will turn into an eventual sale.

If you're a web designer you'd be working on things like client proposals, upselling existing clients, networking with new clients at an event, or selling your packages online through a webinar.

More importantly you need to remember the whole reason you are in business is to make an impact in your clients' lives.

And by reclaiming your time, you can take two months holiday a year to travel the world or simply enjoy time off, while your business runs along smoothly and doesn't require all your time and attention.

Sounds like FREEDOM to me!

Delegate Your Dislikes

Nobody likes doing things they don't like or enjoy. And as an entrepreneur you get to CHOOSE what lights your fire and what it is that you actually enjoy doing.

If you're not having fun in business, as Richard Branson says, you're not doing it right!

In this step, I'd like you to identify which things you're currently doing that you dislike (e.g tweaking your wordpress theme) or shouldn't be doing (e.g customer support) that you could delegate today.

You might have a really long list, and a few of those things that would be EASY to handover to someone who's more than capable of doing them for you, should stand out straight away.

What I want you to keep focusing on is how great you're going to feel when you're no longer managing these pesky tasks that.

1. Don't align with what you're naturally talented at.

2. Suck the life out of you and demotivate you.

I don't want you to fall into the trap of putting this off for another day, or worse yet, telling me that "It's going to take time I don't have to hand these over though Natalie."

My response to that is, yeah sure maybe an extra 10-20 mins out of your day now, so you never have to be doing this again.

As opposed to getting trapped in the mentality that you're the only person who can do this and saying it doesn't take that much time, so I'll just quickly do it again myself.

This is where I suggest you come back to look at your Toggl weekly time tracking results and see that every time you're updating and editing your blog post for example, it's taking you forty five minutes.

That's forty five minutes of your life that you can never get back, working on something you really shouldn't be, instead of focusing on the work you love...or simply going for a gym workout, reading your favourite book, or getting out for a walk in nature.

When you look back on your life I'm pretty sure you won't be saying, "Man I wish I edited more of my blog posts."

Where I see people typically go wrong here is they try to get rid of a task that they haven't really got their head around, or aren't actually doing very well, so they don't hand it off in the right way.

The other common mistake is you don't identify all the things you're automatically doing well, and you miss talking about them when you're delegating.

Which means the process is missing or incomplete from the get go. So whoever you hire to do it for you will do it wrong—and then you will waste a lot of time redoing it yourself.

Let's get them off your plate right away shall we?

Get Your 'A Team' On

Next up is finding the right person to outsource too.

Right about now I want you to take off your 'perfectionist' hat, hang up your, 'I'm the only person who can do this' coat, and instead, look for 'good enough.'

The reason being is that for the first few tasks you delegate, they can be small tasks that will not ruin your business if someone you hire initially gets them wrong.

That rarely happens because you have this awesome SOP to show them exactly how to do it right.

No SOP? No worries, because that's exactly what Chapter 11 is going to show you how to do!

What You Learned In This Chapter:

- Diagnosing where you have superhero syndrome.

- How to identify your time thieves and how much that is costing you.

- The art of delegating your dislikes and reclaiming your time.

10

FINDING, HIRING AND BUILDING YOUR GLOBAL DREAM TEAM

If you're wanting more freedom in your life and business, the first thing you have to do is stop doing everything yourself. You will run yourself into the ground if you think you can manage every single piece of your business, day in and day out.

Then one day you'll get sick, or worse, you'll get burned-out and your business will fall over before your very eyes. You'll realize, you've built your business around yourself. So if you're not around, your business simply doesn't run.

That ain't freedom, and that ain't a business.

The benefits of outsourcing are huge and once you start let me tell you it gets a little bit addictive.

You will actually save more time and make more money once you start building a team, trust me on this.

You get to work on the stuff you love and you get people who are better than you to work on the rest. Also, hiring a full-time GVA (General Virtual Assistant) for forty hours a week will only set you back around US$500 per hire, especially if you use the services that I will share with you in this chapter.

In Chapter 9 I gave you some concrete examples and activities to do to help you identify where you can remove yourself from the business and what to delegate.

Most of us have this inner "control freak syndrome" or perfectionist tendencies that mean we don't think anyone else can do what we are doing better than we can, which is quite often a lie.

Or we're running on a minimal budget and don't think we can afford to hire really talented people, but as I've just proven to you that is also not the case.

We have a lack of knowledge on how to go about hiring the right person and limited time to train and trust new team members and I get it. But some of the tools that I am going to show you and the way in which you can use them these days, makes it so much easier for you.

You Don't Have To Be An HR Department

Typically some of the things that are really easy to start off with, are research projects, or hiring a Virtual Assistant to help you with formatting your blog, even doing some small html coding edits on your website if you trust them enough.

Maybe you want them to take over your calendar scheduling. Perhaps they will be researching and writing blog posts for you. Think of just one thing that you can start handing off and then I'm going to show you how to go about making a hire.

If you're sitting on the fence, heed the wise words of Matt McWilliams, mattmcwilliams.com

> "You'll never have true freedom in your business, until you learn to delegate and let go.
>
> If you control everything and micromanage, you aren't an entrepreneur and you don't have freedom. You just own your job.

Here's the key thing I learned, no one will ever do a task exactly like I want it done. And that is OK. Half the time they'll do it better. 45% of the time they'll do it well enough. And 5% of the time they'll mess up.

No mistake is fatal. No mistake is worth me having to micromanage. No mistake has ever cost me more than $10,000.

This is probably the most important lesson I've learned in my business and in life. It has meant all the freedom in the world to me."

The Smart Way To Hire

I am a big fan of asking my friends and peers for referrals in their network of smart, talented people they know or work with, when I'm first looking to hire someone for my team.

However, if you want to get started quickly and test out several potential contractors, I highly recommend you sign up to the wonderful site called, Upwork, one of the world's largest online global communities of skilled freelancers.

An alternative is Remote.com or if you're on a tight budget you could start with fiverr.com too where small jobs start from US$5.

When you login to Upwork you can:

- Look at what types of jobs are being advertised.

- Search for freelancers.

- Interview or hire someone on the spot.

- Run reports once you start having a tea.

- Message your entire team and manage them.

- Look at your contractor's time diary.

This platform has it all. You can search by industry or the experience you need. And let's say you want to build an app, you can go to the Web and mobile and software development section, and within that there's game development, product management, Q&A testing and web development.

For an administrative role you can narrow it down to admin support, data entry, project management, transcription, web research and more.

There are literally tons of different areas for you to look at and find exactly what you want done. Then once you have a role in mind that you want to outsource, you can simply post a job. They will walk you through it, it's really easy.

If you've done a job before you can reuse past ones anytime. You simply give the title of the role that you are looking for, then you choose the category. Is it web development? Is it administration? is it writing? You describe the work to be done so have a look at a couple of swipe files that are included with this module for starters.

But essentially, what you are wanting to do here is cut and paste your job description and you really can't be too clear or give too much detail in terms of explanation of exactly what you'd like done.

You can then list the skills that are needed. For example, are they going to be using Adobe Photoshop?

Do they need to be professional in Asana, in MailChimp?

Then you can either choose to pay them by the hour or on a weekly rate, or even a retainer or a one-off contract fee.

So if you know your budget is $10 an hour, you can set it at that. If you know you only have $200 for an entire project, then you can set a project rate and then people actually will bid for your project.

Then you can estimate the duration of the contract. Is this going to be ongoing for say 5, 10,15, 20 hours per week or is this going to be a one off project? Do you need somebody for three months? Tons of flexibility on here.

You can also qualify the best candidates so you can say, "I want an entry level person or I want an expert." You get to choose.

For example, I would want a copywriter that is an intermediate expert. I would probably want a web designer that's an intermediate expert or when it comes to data entry, or administration for example, I am potentially looking for somebody who I can train up from an entry level.

You can choose the marketplace visibility that you want and you can suggest how many people you would actually like to hire for the job. Also, I suggest you do when you first start up, is hire two people to do the same task. Then you can pit them against each other and you may want to take both of them on.

I did this with a research project where I ended up taking on two Virtual Assistants because they both did a great job. In another task I took on the one person who'd far outshone the other.

I spent $20 for a couple of hours of their time to do some research and data entry for me, and from there they went on and worked with me in other ways on different tasks.

You can attach a document if you've already written up a wonderful job description or you have supporting resources that are going to help them make a decision. You can add in qualifications so if there is a specific skill they need - for example HTML and Java experience - then you can also add that in there.

You can ask them to write you a cover letter if this is important, because if you want them to be doing your customer service, they need to be able to write and explain things correctly and speak in a great language and be really conversant.

Then, if you want to put out a cover letter so you can test their English and the way they write and communicate. You can even put in screening questions.

The minute you post this job it goes live and you will get many candidates applying.

I hired somebody within an hour. I put up a job description. It got about 60 applications to it. I scrolled down based on the qualification and the skills that I wanted them to have and their ratings. I cut out a ton of people.

This left about ten.

I went through all their resumes and CVs and made a hire on the spot without interviewing because the role wasn't super important. It wasn't critical work that needed to be done by an expert.

Start With The Right Candidates And Fit Them To The Best Roles

If you don't want to post a job, you can connect with freelancers directly, then discuss the role in question you think they're best suited for.

When you do your search you get such granular information for example,

> *Mary Shane is an expert in admin support and accurate encoder. She is based in the Philippines. Her skills are Adobe Photoshop and administrative support. She's currently charging $5 an hour. She's done 17,080 hours of work on UpWork. She's done the*

'Upward Office Skills test' and got in the top 20% on a Word test. Plus she has 100% job success.

From her profile I can see she did really well on her english basic skill test, where she was above average and her spelling test was below average. In this case I would look to assign her roles where she wasn't necessarily writing copy or editing blog posts, but she might be fine communicating with my customers. This would depend on how good her english is, which I'd establish when I interview her.

Upwork shows you all the jobs that she's had as well as her education. From there you can either save and come back to her at a later date or you can contact her and get in touch and say, "Hey! I'd like to know more about XYZ." or "I've got this job that I've posted that I am directing you to."

Or you could actually just hire her straight away, especially if you've already got a job set up and you invite her to apply for your job.

At this point let's say we are going to go to admin support and I'm going to pick transcription and I can assign the title 'Excellent Transcriptionist.'

You can then select whether you want to pay an hourly rate or a fixed price and say what our exact budget is - for example $40. You can say exactly when the work is due and share instructions for them to get started. This is best done by attaching a role description as a file so they can hit the ground running.

If you need to get something transcribed, this is how quickly you can do it.

Example In Action: Dr Alexis Shields

Dr. Alexis Shields is a Naturopathic doctor who works 100% virtually via dralexisshields.com

She helps executives and management teams around the world increase productivity and improve their brain and body performance by doing in-depth assessments of their blood work. Healthy people are more productive and happier at work, and this translates to increasing the bottom line.

Over the last two years, Alexis has built her online practice mostly by word of mouth and by being a guest on podcasts, and is now working on a more strategic sales funnel to scale her business.

She has a small team of two virtual assistants (VAs) who are very much part-time.

> "After going through a number of Vas, it finally dawned on me that I should contact the medical school that I went to to find a student. They would be eager and knowledgeable.
>
> So now I have a student who has been with me for the last 1.5 years and she has been a saving grace for my business and my sanity. She's freed me up to work more on what I love - learning how to be a great doctor for my clients.
>
> I recently hired another VA from Romania. She has done small tasks for me in the past (found on UpWork) and I kept going back to her because she was reliable. I finally hired her on and she has been incredible."

So what does Alexis outsource, given her work is so specialised?

> "We do a lot of data transfer from labs all over the world to a google doc spreadsheet that I create for each client, which

organizes all of their data so that we can see their health trends over time and if their labs are in the optimal health ranges.

My VAs also help with emailing and basic clerical stuff - writing SOPs on our systems, emailing with clients who need to get their follow up testing done, need help scheduling, billing etc. Basically, what a front desk would do in the typical medical office.

Hiring has contributed to increasing my income by 30% this year and it has allowed me to focus more on clients and outreach rather than clerical tasks."

Alexis likes to keep things small, even though she's planning on doubling her business this year. She may look to add on another doctor to do consults when her schedule is full, but she doesn't want to be in the business of managing a big team.

Alexis' goal is to scale to high six figures with a small team consisting of her, her two virtual assistants and the occasional graphic designer/video editor contract.

She's clear on what she wants and how much she wants to take on, because remember, the more people you have, even with the right systems and tools in place, the more time you will spend leading and managing your team.

Sylvia van de Logt is the founder of 40plusstyle.com and has become savvy with her team and delegating.

"I'm constantly looking for new ways to outsource and automate. I started 40+entrepreneurs, where I want to help women over 40 give the confidence and knowledge to start their own online business and enjoy some of the financial freedom I have.

Outsourcing is helping me achieve this goal. First off, it gives me more time to focus on growing the business. The only way to do that is through building a good team and systems that can run the business without me. I'm very much the face of the business though, so I will always play a key role at the front end.

I was cruising quite nicely for a few years, making good money, until I realised that growth was minimal and that I was basically doing the same things each day.

When I started out it was just a little revenue from Adsense and affiliate commissions. Then I added in eBooks and with more traffic everything grew. When I started, my goal was to make at least $3,000 per month, but now my goal is much higher.

I had resisted the idea of outsourcing quite a bit, (as I don't like to be a manager) but I realised that I could only grow if I took myself out of the business more and started creating systems and hire people to do some of the many tasks I do on a daily basis."

She recruited an expert stylist who also manages the member community. She also hired a senior editor who now manages most of the content for 40plusstyle.com.

In addition she has contractors who do the bookkeeping, write occasional articles, help with web design and development, do editing for the upcoming 40+Entrepreneur podcast and she has a full time virtual assistant. She is now looking to hire a marketing assistant as well.

"Having an expert stylist for my style club and a good editor for 40+Style, saves me a LOT of time, which I can spend on developing programs instead and create sales funnels. Just by adding the membership offering in early 2017 I added $2,500 to monthly revenue. I would have not been able to create it without help from my team."

Her business now makes a five figure income every month.

"My virtual assistant helps with the nitty gritty tasks, which also saves me time. I have an online blogger community list that people can submit to. Submission is automatic through an online form that adds people to my list. It goes into Helpscout, my VA now adds people to the lists once a month.

I conduct regular interviews with stylish 40+ bloggers. That's now fully taken care of my VA, who also completes many of my blog posts. My writers or I write them, but she does all the alt tagging, social media scheduling (in co-schedule), makes sure affiliate links are put in, optimizes the post and creates the featured images.

She also helps me source comparable products to the fashion items I feature and creates shop the post widgets and shoppable boutiques. I work with a photographer who takes pictures in New York and she turns these images into blog posts. And she…

- Resizes and optimises images.

- Approves and checks people in my groups.

- Helps with creating my online trainings

- Puts together weekly throwback Thursday articles.

- Selects and schedules many of my pinterest pins (through Tailwind).

- Updates online boutiques and checks regularly that links in popular articles are still working.

- Creates new style collages.

- Sources photos and comments from my groups, which I turn into articles and interviews.

- Provides customer support to our members.

- Compiles business reports.

My editor (who is English):

- Writes and schedules articles.

- Does keyword research and comes up with article ideas.

- Manages the editorial calendar.

- Updates social media.

- Creates boutiques.

- Photographs herself and makes collages.

- Monitors Facebook groups and adds frequent posts to groups.

- Uploads updates through buffer.

- Creates and uploads Facebook Live videos.

- Creates Youtube videos.

- Helps with newsletters to 40+Style and member club.

- Helps with online meetings and webinars.

- Interviews specialists and schedules interviews.

- Liaises with advertisers.

- Helps with customer support.

All communication with my team is through Asana and coschedule."

———

As you can see Sylvia has, overtime, delegated a lot of tasks that are now handled by her team, freeing her up to do what she loves. As you get to trust your team members, and better understand their skills, you can upgrade their role to suit your growing business.

Toby Jenkins at Bluewire Media has dealt with hiring and managing a lot of team members. After many years of learning what worked well, and what truly didn't, he suggests.

> "The Topgrading screening phone call (before you offer an interview) is the key tool I use. It takes five minutes and has only four questions. Read "Who" by Geoff Smart to get all the other hiring gold you need but here are the screening questions.
>
> - What are your career goals?
>
> - What are you really good at professionally?
>
> - What are you not good at or not interested in doing professionally?
>
> - Who were your last five bosses, and how <u>will</u> they each rate your performance on a 1-10 scale <u>when</u> we talk to them?"

Other hiring tips from Toby are…

1. Use your probation period wisely and be sure you don't let it just slip past without really evaluating whether both the business and the employee are getting the value you both want. On the people front it's a, "hell yeah" or not at all. Ultimately, it's really hard to know whether someone is a good fit, until you've worked with them for a while.

2. Read "Who" by Geoffrey Smart before you hire anyone. The Topgrading Methodology is excellent!

3. Small weekly check-ins with team members is far more useful than

massive yearly ones. Catch problems early when they're easy to solve and learn people's strengths to evolve their roles.

Tools To Manage Your Sexy Team

While I cover the best of the best tools in the next chapter, let's run through some of the tools I recommend to communicate with and manage your team way more effectively.

I love these tools so much and so do my team.

- Asana for task and project management. You can also try Trello.

- Slack for team communication or simply go with What's App or Telegram.

- Google Apps for managing and sharing documents. One Drive is good too.

- Zapier for getting your tools to talk to each other.

1. Asana

This awesome to-do list and project management tool can be used by you for your personal life, for your business and for your team.

It's free too and the interface is fantastic. To get started, you simply set up a task, a description, due date and assignee (you or someone on your team) and you're off and running.

That's just the basics. The real capability in Asana lies in the ability to create Projects, and within a project, tasks and subtasks.

Templates are also brilliant for taking a blueprint from a past project or task to easily copy and repurpose for new projects/tasks.

For example, our entire Editorial Calendar SOP is an Asana template that can be duplicated, and optimized for any other SOP we choose to create.

Every step of the SOP becomes a task or subtask in Asana for each action that needs to be taken.

Example In Action: Publishing A Blog Post

- First step goes to my content manager to write a draft blog post.

- Next, I'm assigned a subtask to edit and check and it.

- Then, my assistant is assigned a subtask to load the final blog post into our WordPress site, format it and make it SEO friendly.

- Then my assistant will create the blog image.

- Next task for is for my content manager or myself to check all of this and publish.

- This then triggers the appropriate social media sharing using Buffer

As each person does their bit, they can then set the deadline for the next person. We also comment on a task if someone has a question or needs help. Everything is contained within this project, and within the tasks.

You can add attachments too, which are especially handy when we are signing off designs for products, adverts and logos as well as content - links to Google Docs or actual files are all easy to attach, and they're then linked via Asana.

Asana is focused on ACTION, while for us, detailed plans are stored in Google Drive. If something needs to be done, it goes in Asana.

It's a great tool for centralizing communication for specific projects and tasks, and serves as a portal to the rest of the business. Also, it eliminates the need for email, which is brilliant. No tasks or requests ever get emailed now, so there's no chance of things being lost in an email thread split between multiple people.

I highly suggest you turn Asana email notifications off, and get into the practice of checking your Asana inbox each morning instead.

What I love about it, is you can view your inbox for updates on what your team is doing, and where they're at and what they are working on. You can also view just your own tasks, by due date or priority. It really gets you focused on what matters.

It is important to have best practices that are regularly enforced so it's a reliable source of information, otherwise people can use Asana in different ways. Everyone has to be on board and make it their main tool. This took us about a month, until people were comfortable, and now it works brilliantly.

2. Google Drive

This is my home. Every single thing I need is stored in a series of clearly labeled folders. I have a Google Drive for my personal needs and for my Business(es).

All documents, videos, audio files, graphics and course content are stored in the appropriate folders.

Detailed plans, including launch strategies, financials, weekly reports are stored as a living, breathing google doc, spreadsheet, slides or forms.

The sharing ability of Google Drive is perhaps one of the most useful features. You can share documents or spreadsheets you're working on with anyone.

If you are set up on Google Suite and paying for your own email addresses linked to your domain, and paying for extra storage, then you can share a file or a folder with just the people in your organization, or individuals.

Once more, you can make the link viewable to people who have it, or to the public. You can also choose whether people can view only, view and comment or edit. So you control the access.

This is super handy if you're writing a proposal or launch document, and need people to leave comments only, or only share editing rights with a handful of people.

It also means, if you have an online course or content you can host the files in Google Drive and share the link with them via email or the course platform from Google directly. Anytime you update that file or content, the link stays the same, and everyone who has access automatically sees the latest revision or version.

You can store up to 30GB of data on Google Drive for free, after that it's ridiculously affordable to increase your storage into several terabytes. It's negated the need for me to use Dropbox anymore, and realistically to use a backup hard drive.

Plus, it links to every other Google product including gmail, analytics, calendar etc. It's your business in one powerful package, it's free to start, and grows with your needs.

3. Slack

I like to think of Slack as your instant messenger with a purpose. For any real-time chats, sharing of resources that are useful like a great blog post, or a how to video that will help the team.

It's also useful to share wins and successes, update everyone at once with the latest news, private messaging between team members (or clients if you use it for that), as well as discussing a task at hand.

It's not a tool for delegating - all that should go into Asana - but it's great for keeping in touch, quick answers to questions and collaborating with one or many people.

Slack let's you have Public Channels that everyone you've invited to your Slack can see. For us we have #general, #ideastoaction and #tooltips.

You can also have Private Channels that you can invite just a few key people to, this may relate to a project you're working on, or a product.

You can have as many Slack Dashboards as you wish.

I have one for SuitcaseEntrepreneur.com and Right2Freedom.com and would start one for any new business. You can also be invited to other people's Slacks, so if you have several clients who are using it, you can join theirs and be part of the conversations.

Warning: I like to minimize the invitations I get and am selective about what I join, otherwise, you'd spend all day in Slack responding to new updates, depending on how big a team or project is and how many people are using it.

It's useful for just about anyone, but especially agencies, coaches and consultants, who use it to invite their clients to private channels to communicate more regularly with them and stay on track of projects.

All of these apps have both a desktop and mobile app, which I adore as I often, single-handedly run my business from my mobile using them, anytime, anywhere.

4. Zapier

Zapier moves info between your web apps automatically, so you can focus on your most important work. It integrates with apps like Facebook, Slack, Quickbooks, Google Docs, Google Sheets, XERO and so many more.

What it does is cut down your workflow and repetitive tasks into Zaps. For example, you can set up a Zap to say.

Trigger: When I get a new email in Gmail.

Action: Copy the attachment from Gmail to Google Drive.

Action: Alert me in Slack about the new Google Drive file.

You can see how helpful this can be. You can set up Zaps for virtually anything. Once more, Zapier provides you with Zaps to copy and use for yourself.

Again, this tool is free for a certain amount of Zaps, after which there's a nominal monthly fee.

Building A Team Around Your Company Vision

As your business grows and you release control of every aspect, you need a company culture plan of action in place so your vision continues to come to life through your team.

A lot of people ask me…

- How do you go about creating longevity?

- How do you keep people on in your team and motivated?

- Are they going to leave me straight away?

- What if I don't trust them?

All of these questions are completely normal to ask, and I know it's scary taking on your first hire, but it's also just as daunting for your twentieth hire. The same questions do crop up, even after years of experience, because we're dealing with people here, and everyone is different.

I can't say I'm the expert in this area, but what I do know for sure is…

- **Treat your team members as you'd like to be treated** and empower them to make decisions on your behalf.

- **Be patient** (something I have to constantly work on) and take time to expertly communicate what you're delegating to your team. When they don't understand, evaluate what you could do in the future to communicate it in a better way and then stick consistently with what's working.

- **Spend quality time with your team,** especially if you're a virtual team. It's understandably harder to catch up when you span international timezones, but regular weekly or at least monthly full team video meetings, using Zoom for example, make a huge difference. You can also look to host a team retreat on to two times per year, where you get together, cultivate relationships further, offer education during that time and make plans for the next 6-12 months of business.

- **Encourage feedback and opinions**. Your team is the best source of feedback that you have. Encourage honesty and foster each person's natural talent to generate ideas so you can continually build your business off of human innovation that understands your vision.

- **Don't micromanage**. Most people wouldn't think it's possible to hover over someone's shoulder, while on a virtual team, but it is. Trust that once you've conveyed the message that it's been understood, set a due date, use your tools and trust in your systems. If it's not what you wanted, communicate why and detail how it could be fixed in the future with as much patience as you can muster up.

Set your intentions from the start, communicate them to your team, and I guarantee you'll have a stronger team that feels like a major factor to your company instead of another cog in a machine.

From A Logistical Standpoint You Must:

- Make sure you get them to sign a simple contract outlining their role description and what's expected (Upwork has a great contract built-in, that you both agree to before hiring) or you can use ContractExpress.com

- Have each team member sign an Non Disclosure Agreement, (NDA) which protects you and your intellectual property from being used down the line, or your work popping up somewhere six months later.

Sure, there are horror stories out there about people who worked with freelancers, who they didn't trust or they stole some of their intellectual property or they took their website down.

I have certainly had that happen to me, but at the end of the day I put trust in the people I hire. That they will do a great job for me. That I will treat them well and we will work well together.

And a big part of why I think the reason for my success in the last few years is that I've been sharing Life Canva (my three year vision) with every team member who comes on board.

I cover this fully in the Freedom Plan program as it's such a powerful tool.

It's basically a clear vision of what you want your life and business to look, feel, and be like three years from now, but written in the present tense. It is a very powerful exercise to do.

Plus, having that vision in place, instills an energy in the team because they become just as excited as you are about the future of your company, especially when you convey it in the most open, genuine way possible.

One of the worst things you can do is to disempower your team. You want to inspire and empower them, and have them feel like they own the company and your vision as much as you do.

Straight away, when they start working with me, they get sent my Life Canvas so they know what our mission is, and what we are working towards. The rest of my systems and procedures I share with you in Chapter 11.

Two Words That Will Transform Your Team

Your team must buy into your vision to make it become a reality. Then they must have the autonomy to do their best job.

One of my favourite tips I've ever received is from my friend Laura Roeder, who uses two words to empower her team members, and to take responsibility for their work when they have a question. She simply says 'Your Call'.

She transformed her business, simply by replying to emails, or endless questions, with these two words. And it worked. People on her team stepped back, and thought about what action they'd take in this situation if they owned the business. They would then email her saying, "I'd do this" and she'd say, "Great, so would I, so go ahead and make that happen."

I think the key reason why people have trouble from time to time with taking on new hires is, they don't clearly articulate where that person fits into the team, why the work that they do is important, even if it's initial administrative stuff, it's still really helping you out.

It's saving you time and energy, it's allowing you to do more of the work that you want to do and that is a huge asset to have them on your team.

So keep telling them, keep complimenting them, keep telling them when they are doing a great job and it's going to be better for everyone.

However, you need to acknowledge and address when something isn't going well, or isn't up to standard, and you need to do this immediately.

It's better to be clear and out in the open and upfront, not to sit on something and fester and let it get worse.

It will cost each of you more time, money and heartache that isn't necessary.

Now, it's time to create your own outsourcing plan and go to Upwork to make your first hire.

If you've never hired before, start with the first team member you really need that can plug that gap in your daily activities and make a huge difference to your workload (and sanity). Then look at the next task on your list you 'don't want to do' or 'shouldn't be doing' and do the same, hire to fill that role.

As you outsource more and more, it can become ridiculously addictive once you start freeing up your time, and realize you get to work on the stuff you love, while your awesome team get to work on the other tasks that are critical to your business, but not necessarily what YOU should be doing.

Then you can carry on hiring strategically to grow your business as your budget increases. I know for sure that the more I spend on my team and outsourcing, the more money I make in my business.

What You Learned In This Chapter:

- How to make smart hires on a budget.

- Where to find great freelancers and contractors.

- Examples in action of how to hire and what to handover.

- The best way to build a cohesive team who buy into your vision.

- Tools to lead and manage your team from anywhere.

I want you to go for it and make your first hire or add a new person to your team that's going to take over some of those tasks that you just don't want to be doing and enjoy.

11

SMART SYSTEMS TO STREAMLINE YOUR DAILY OPERATIONS

Systems may not sound enticing, but they are your best friend when it comes to giving you more time, more money, and more freedom to do what you love.

They can transform not only your business, but your life and create daily flow.

A system is a procedure, process, method, or course of action designed to achieve a specific result.

If you're committed to implementing smart, savvy systems that result is freedom in your business.

You can start small and grow from there, but you're going to want to figure out exactly what's holding you back in your business and create a system to solve it.

Let me bring you into a whole new world of productivity, efficiency, peace of mind and calm amidst the chaos of running a business.

Whether you're a solopreneur, or a business owner (AKA with a team), you all need systems for yourself and your business.

Benefit #1: Your Online Business Can Scale Much Faster

Many online businesses become stagnant after a while and fail to grow because they do not have the right systems in place before they're needed.

You may be at that stage right now or heading there, but perhaps you're overwhelmed by the cost, time and effort to implement.

Well let me tell you, I feel you, but know that once your system is in place, the return on your investment is immense.

All those repetitive tasks that take up so much of your time, all the things you keep having to do that you dislike, but there's not way to easily hand it over. Plus, that feeling of running around in circles and never feeling on top of your operations....that will all be taken care of by your friendly systems.

Sure, you will need to pay for a new tool or service and learn how to use these it, or train your team members to do so. But the payoff is huge. Once the systems are in place, your online business will be running like a well-oiled machine.

The phrase, 'make money while you sleep 24/7' will no longer be some marketing gimmick you loathe, it will be your reality. You'll wonder why you didn't do this ages ago.

Benefit #2: You Get To Be The CEO, Not The Manager

A big issue with many entrepreneurs is, feeling like they have to do everything themselves. I am guilty of this myself.

I mean, how could we *not* feel this way? The business is our baby, after all.

But this attachment also leads to getting overwhelmed when the business grows and we realize we are doing more harm than good by not having those important systems in place.

We become focused on ensuring the day-to-day operations are running smoothly, we don't have any time to dedicate to growing or planning for the future.

We tend to keep on doing things just the way we've always done them because this is what we know best. This need to always be in control, only leads us to become ineffective and stops us from scaling or even delegating work.

That is why every online business needs systems in place to ensure that day-to-day operations are running as smoothly as possible.

I would even say that *it is your responsibility* to ensure that you are doing the things necessary to grow your business.

It is up to you to delegate as much of the administrative and process oriented tasks to the systems available to you.

It will allow you to move on from being a manager and become a CEO for your business.

In the end, **systemizing your business will help you to stop trading time for money** and even increase your value by letting you focus on the most important tasks in your business that only you can do.

What Systems Do You Need For Your Online Business Right Now?

These days you can find an app, tool, or system for whatever business task you can imagine. Which is fantastic, until it gets overwhelming just trying to choose which one is best.

As entrepreneurs, our perfectionist tendencies mean we can get stuck for a long time, considering and evaluating all the options.

But the truth is, you are already using some systems even if you aren't aware of it.

- If you have a website, you're probably using WordPress or Squarespace (or something similar), so you don't have to write each line of code to put up a simple, about page.

- If you are collecting email addresses, you are most certainly using an email service provider like ConvertKit or Mailchimp, so you don't have to enter each subscriber's email address into a spreadsheet manually.

- If you have regular meetings with clients or prospects, you are using some version of a calendar tool (Google, iCal, Outlook, Calendly, etc.) to schedule them.

- And if you are accepting online payments, I can almost guarantee you are using Paypal. And if you're a little more advanced, Google Checkout, Amazon Payments or Stripe

These are all systems that we don't pay much attention to. We take them for granted because they work so seamlessly in the background. That's the beauty of smart systems. They make tedious tasks effortless for you.

But the truth is, many of these systems didn't even exist 10-15 years ago. In fact, running a business entirely online had not even occurred to people, until the late 1990s.

Technology has grown by leaps and bounds since then, but the basics of building a business have not changed at all. And even though there are systems available to help you run your online business, you don't need all of them.

To help you decide which parts of your online business you can systemize, try answering the following questions?

- Are there any repetitive tasks that I have to do daily/weekly?

- What things do I need to remember and recall frequently? (Ever forgot your password, anyone?)

- What are the tasks that I absolutely hate doing, and would rather have someone else do?

- What tasks should I not be doing that I could delegate to someone else?

- Are the numbers (of leads, transactions, emails, etc.) so large that I just can not deal with them manually anymore?

- Which parts of my business could be fully automated? (There's a good chance that someone has already created a system for it).

- Where am I spending most of my time daily and how can I optimize it?

- What systems do I need to grow my business?

I have tried hundreds of tools and systems over the last 10 years of running my businesses. And as a location independent, these tools and systems have been indispensable in running my business.

So let's break this down into three key areas to focus on.

1. Operations

2. SOPS

3. Tools

Operations

What does this actually mean? In my mind, it's the heart that pumps continuously, or the engine that runs 24 hours and keeps everything ticking.

It provides all the working parts with fuel and can keep on going, even when you're not around to monitor it.

It's also something most freelancers and entrepreneurs ignore, until they start getting more organized, truly understand what it is their business does, and realize how important it is.

What I'm really talking about here is a set of operating guidelines, with which, to run your business and your team, that you could give to a complete stranger and they'd be able to read it and understand it, and likely put it to work straight away.

In his book, *Work the System*, Sam Carpenter talks about the simple mechanics of making more and working less. And this comes from systems, and systems are built from an operational foundation.

> "Here's the no-brainer that eludes most people. In the course of a day and in the course of a life, each movement we make is a single step in a linear sequence of steps intended to accomplish one or another goal. *Each thing we do is a component of a system, a system that has purpose.*
>
> You are a project engineer and you direct the events of the day; you're not a leaf blowing in the wind.

Although, I'm sure you may be reading this and thinking to yourself, 'Actually Natalie I am!'

That's ok. In fact, it's perfectly natural. I don't believe at anytime in our life, at school or University or with our parents or friends, are we made to take a step back and look at what we do as a series of linear systems.

Sure, each of those events and experiences in our life that happened as we grew up and got educated, and had work experience, have helped, but until you run your own business, you simply can't fathom the many moving parts and activities you're going to need to get a handle on.

As Sam Carpenter wisely states.

"First, *it's what done does that counts.* Good intentions and a positive attitude are not enough. Really, thoughts don't even matter. What matters is the action one takes, right here in the tangible world.

Second, *getting things right most of the time is good enough.* The things that don't come out well are just part of the overhead. The cost of doing business, of taking risks, of external confusion, of coping with events that are sometimes one step ahead of your best efforts, of being alive.

As by-products of your advancement forward, accept that less-than-perfect events are going to happen."

This is definitely true, and most people don't fail from making mistakes, they fail because they don't take action, which is my favourite thing to do. In fact, I live by Yoda's quote: *Do or do not. There is no try.*

What often happens is we dive into a business. Much like diving in the deep end and learning to swim, without ever stopping to analyze our swimming technique, where we could make changes or improve to get more speed in the water, more efficiency and less friction.

So if you've been struggling to swim in the deep end, take my hand, and I'll pull you out of the water, and into the crystal blue calm shallow waters of systems.

Your Master Operations Manual

Have your eyes glazed over yet? Well open them wide as the Master Operations Manual is an awesome, succinct document that covers your whole business at a glance.

You can create it yourself or with your team, or even a coach and the more organization you have in your business, the easier it is.

It acts as the starting document I'd send to any new contractor or employee joining my business, to give them the complete overview of the who, what, when and why, and gets them settled in.

If you head to thefreedomplan.co/start   you will get a FREE template for this document sent to you, that you can edit to your heart's content.

I've adapted and tweaked this template from the one that my fellow freedom systems friend Mandi Effelson originally adapted from Tropical MBA and Work the System, to create this version.

Most people learn best by example, so I'm going to share some our manual to give you an idea.

We cover 7 areas: Mission | Principles | Team | Operations | Products | Content and Technology.

What you cover in yours is completely up to you and dependent on your business. It all starts with the strategic overview or mission.

Mission

Insert your mission, ours is…

> In 5 years from now, we will have helped 100,000 + people achieve more personal daily freedom, live a life they love, and have the time, money and freedom to do that every single day. We want to be a little breath of fresh air in their day that brings them joy, happiness and freedom by providing the tools, strategies, habits and resources to achieve this.

General Operation Principles

Then you dive into your general operating principles. For example, our first three of seven are…

1. Our business focuses first on helping humans transform their mindset, habits and therefore, their lives. We use this as a litmus test for all of our actions and resulting procedures.

2. **Our customers are WAY more important than our prospects**. We focus on "inside out" marketing. We focus our energy on getting great information and education to our community and letting them spread the word about our products and services because they love them.

3. We 'do it now.' When inspiration strikes, we don't overplan. We visualize the best possible outcome. Decide on the first two steps. Clear our desks, focus, and ship.

Team

Next up, your team, and this is a great place to be able to clearly define each and every person on your team starting with YOU, your title, what you do and what you are the go to person for.

In our manual, it starts with me as the Chief Freedomist, then my virtual assistant, Chief of happiness and marketing, audio and video editor, graphic designer, WordPress consultant and web designer and my Facebook Ads specialist.

These people are the core of my team, although none of them are full time and they are all contractors.

Operations And Expectations

For operations and expectations, list out your regular operations activities, and each team member's role and what they do, for example we have.

Rolly

Title: Audio/Video Editor

Rolly is your go-to for: Video and audio editing needs

Role & responsibilities: Podcast, vlog, course modules

Superpower: Attention to detail

We include internal links to the relevant SOP (standard operating procedures) folders for each area of our business, such as, *how to edit, publish and promote the podcast*, followed by our internal communication expectations where we talk about our tools and how we best use them.

We also cover external communication expectations, availability and notice, how and when to invoice me and payment options.

Products And Services

We decided to add in a section called products just because there are several within my business and anybody new coming in might be slightly overwhelmed or confused!

So we break each product down with.

- A small snippet on what the program or project is called.

- A short description on what it is and what's included.

- What's the background on it?

- What is the current status?

- The future plans and a link to that particular product on our website.

In this section, we also include a link to our *Plan of attack and editorial calendar*, as well as where the podcast folder is located on Google Drive, blog posts, mega posts and social media.

You will find this immensely helpful to get a big picture view of your own business, as well as making it super easy and efficient for any new hire to understand where they fit in and where everything can be found.

Technology

The last two sections are technology - the key tools we use to run a business and how we use them. I share those in this chapter below for you to emulate.

That's it. That is your Operations Manual to make you feel like a Boss, and make your team feel like they know what the heck is going on at all times!

2. SOPS (Smart Operating Procedures)

In the real world, they call these Standard Operating Procedures, but since that bores me to even reading it, I've replaced it with the word smart. Because life and business should be fun and smart.

What is it you may ask?

Basically, it's an exact breakdown of a task from start to finish that anybody should be able to follow if they read it.

The point of it is that it should be so clear that ANYONE could open up this document and follow the steps and be able to do it.

Creating your first or 50th SOP feels so freeing, once you've finally documented what the heck it is you want to handover and get off your plate!

And it shouldn't take you long. No really it shouldn't. Let me show you how.

How To Create An SOP In Less Than Five Minutes

The next time you do or are about to do, one of the tasks you've written down that you dislike or shouldn't be doing (you know one you do every day), you do the following task at the SAME time.

Let's Take This Made-Up Example (Based On A Real World Person).

Juan runs a cloud based accounting service and likes to treat his clients as VIPs. Every single time he signs a new client it's a pretty manual process.

He goes into his CRM system and creates a new contact, tags them appropriately so he can find them in a search and categorizes what level of payment they're on plus the terms of their contract based on what package they chose.

Each time this takes him maybe 10-12 minutes, depending on the level of complexity involved or details he needs to enter in.

But with several new clients coming on board, each day it adds up to over five hours of admin during a week that he could be putting towards doing the actual work for his clients.

And therefore, the next time he does this, he goes to Loom.com, a free tools that records your screen. He starts a recording of him talking over the top of what he's doing on the screen.

By short, I mean five to ten minutes. So Juan would show how to login, how to create a new contact, and the details you need to enter in etc.

My suggestion is you do what it is you need to do to a certain point, so Juan could show a mainly completed contact, with everything pre-filled in, then record from there with any additional tips and tricks, like shortcuts or tagging or processes, that are important to do every time.

Then, he simply ends the video and presto - he has his SOP and a handy link to copy and send via email or slack to his team member so they can watch instantly.

Continue to do this for five to ten tasks (including your inbox) over the space of a week and you'll be amazed at how many tasks you can create SOPs for and therefore hand off to someone else!

You can also use Zoom.com - my tool of choice for running team meetings, group coaching, and interviews in both video and audio, plus screen sharing, recording and even webinars.

BONUS: To get a copy of my handy SOP template and example, simply sign up to the free course at thefreedomplan.co/start

Why Don't People Do This?

Because it takes time and initial effort. Moreover, it means getting out of the habit of doing your usual 'routine task' and this time actually recording or documenting it.

I believe the reason people don't do that is because deep down it makes it a reality that you are actually GOING to delegate this task and relinquish control - something you desperately want to do but also find kind of scary.

Focus on how great you'll feel as you get all these tasks off your plate so you can focus on what you love doing!

I do these all the time now, whenever I am learning something new, or using a new tool. Better yet, I get my team to do it instead, especially if they've discovered a new feature in our email client, or Google has updated a feature and we want to use it.

I simply empower my team with the two words, 'Your Call' to go and update our existing SOPs that are in Google Drive under their own folder called, wait for it, 'SOPS.'

Go the subfolder within that folder, for example, Email, ConvertKit, Teachable, ClickFunnels, Podcast, Wordpress - and update the relevant SOP google doc.

These are living, breathing documents that anyone should be able to update at any time, when a best practice is made even better, or we eliminate or add in steps.

Of course the SOP folder is linked to in the Operations Manual so people can easily be directed to the repository of wonderful instructions for the important tasks that drive our business.

So let's dive into some of my favourites to make your life easier, shall we?

3. Tools

If I had to run my business from just a few key tools, quite honestly, I think I could get away with simply using a payment system, like Paypal or Stripe and social media.

How? On social media I could be promoting my products and services and I could lead them off to a simple Paypal URL, where they could buy that.

I could even do this just with the phone and a bank account if I was really low-tech!

It doesn't need to be complicated, but of course the more you grow and scale your business, the more complex it often becomes and the more you invest in quality tools with full functionality.

Aside from a laptop and a smartphone, I've covered off on the top ten tools I think are most important for running a secure, streamlined and efficient online business.

#1. Lastpass

This is by far and wide the handiest tool that I've ever found. It's basically the last password that you are ever going to have to remember.

You use your LastPass login details to activate it on your computer or your smartphone device, and then it goes ahead and remembers all your other passwords every single time you are logging in to different sites.

I have over four hundred sites and passwords stored in my account that I never need to remember, because it securely remembers all of them with just one password to login with - on your phone or laptop, or someone else's computer.

It creates secure encrypted passwords instantly for you so that you don't use the same combination of numbers and words for every site - you know you do!

The other cool thing about it is you can categorize your passwords that you've saved and the categories like travel, finance, personal, marketing, learning etc. So you can always just search on a category if you can't remember what the site was that you logged in to.

You can also keep notes within the actual tab where you've saved that password so for example, on my bank account I can put in the international banking code in there so that if I needed to send that to somebody it's right there in the notes for me.

And you can share your login access details to sites securely with team members, without actually sharing the password. It's also free. I think you are going to love it.

#2. Wordpress

For me this is still the gold standard and being able to create beautiful websites and blogs. You can create as many as you want using your favourite themes that have versatile features. You can also install and purchase any number of plugins to extend the functionality further.

WordPress is the ultimate content marketing platform, where I can host and display different businesses, different online sites and different marketing portals for membership or products.

#3. Paypal

As I mentioned, probably the easiest way for you to get paid online ever is Paypal. I used Paypal Pro for many years to accept credit cards and people can pay via Paypal or credit card directly. I now use Stripe for this and recurring payments.

You can create buy now buttons, subscribe buttons, donate buttons, trial subscription buttons etcetera, once you have a business account and business account is free. You can also track all your incoming payments and your outgoing payments. You can send invoices too. Fees for payment processing are pretty much in line with other competitors.

Plus, you can create embed codes to just put a button straight on your site and you can send people email links directly to a Paypal subscription.

#4. Google Drive

This is my favourite cloud storage solution. I can login to it from anybody else's laptop at anytime, and access my entire repository of documents, audios, videos, spreadsheets, presentations and files.

I use Google Drive as the main storage solution for anything that is needed long term, such as, all files for my online courses, products, marketing templates, logos and podcast episodes.

I can share folders and files with my team and allow them to view only, comment or edit. The same applies with customers, family and friends.

You can create a public link that anyone can see who has it, or a private link - or any combination of advanced sharing options.

Also, I have all my screenshots directly transfer to Google Drive, as well as photos from my phone. I love the ease of sending a really huge file to someone, either through a link or simply sharing the folder with them that it's in.

They can do the same for me so when I'm running a retreat or workshops and people are taking photos or videos, they can just drop them straight in there and everybody can access them.

I pay for the annual subscription and get 30GB for just $29. It's also completely accessible from your smartphone with almost full capability as on the desktop.

Google Drive is not just for storing files, but it's also for working on current projects.

It's where my editorial content marketing calendar is, any sales copy that I am working on, blog posts in progress, video scripts, newsletters, retreat itineraries, pricing, budgets etc.

You can also use it to create surveys using Google forms, you can upload spreadsheets, and documents that you are working on offline from your laptop, and then make them active live documents.

If you want to step it up a notch, consider G Suite to have your own dedicated email, more storage and much more functionality.

#5. Asana

It would be hard to write this chapter on systems without mentioning the best one of them all – Asana.

It is one of the best free tools I've ever used to simplify my projects, help me plan my days and weeks, manage my team and organize my business.

You can create as many projects as you'd like. For example, we have the *Editorial calendar* template within its own project.

Asana, lets you comment on tasks, tag team members, upload files and attach things to each task. So it's a great way of keeping everything in one place and keeping track of who is doing what and the status of each of your projects.

I would say, on an average, I save between three hours per week using Asana, to set my own daily tasks as well as those of my team, instead of using emails and other tools to streamline every activity.

This system has been an absolute game changer in my business. These are some of the best features of Asana that I absolutely love.

- Track your team's progress and individual tasks.

- A single dashboard to check status updates and discuss projects.

- Assign tasks to specific team members and set due dates.

- Get rid of all email clutter by getting only the updates you need.

- Use colors and tags to easily identify tasks at a glance.

For full details on how I use Asana, go check out The Ultimate Guide on how to use Asana to become a productivity and task management genius.

Oh and it's free.

#6. Sanebox

One of my favourite tools, bringing back sanity to your email inbox, is Sanebox. What I love about it is it's a piece of software (with a small monthly fee) that 'takes over' your Gmail inbox and runs in the background to train itself to understand what's important and what's not.

After a couple of days it starts to prioritize your most important emails and put the in your inbox, and everything else gets filed into Sane Later (not urgent) or Sane News (for all those pesky newsletters you've subscribed to but don't need to read right now).

It takes away your distractions so you can focus on the priorities. That means the only things in my inbox are important emails like ones from you, ones from my team, ones from people that I want to network and connect with and mastermind with, everything else goes into others folders which I can check at any point.

And you can continue to train Sanebox as you go. You will receive a weekly report of how many hours you've saved - for me it's an average of four hours a week in terms of email management. Since using it I consistently get to inbox zero.

Gmail has since added more features, including a simple snooze button, that acts in a similar way to Sanebox.

My virtual assistant now handles my business email so when I login each day there's even less to deal with. It's so freeing.

#7. ConvertKit

My community and engagement with them, is the most important thing in my business. I use ConvertKit, an email marketing system for professional bloggers and entrepreneurs.

ConvertKit's secret sauce, is its ability to tag and segment customers without creating separate lists. What this means is once someone signs up for my email list, they get tagged according to where they signed up from.

For example, if they showed interest in a productivity product, I can set up ConvertKit to send them emails related to productivity and time management.

If they showed interest in location independence, I could send them emails about digital nomads and the freedom lifestyle. And I don't have to do any of this myself! ConvertKit will take care of it automatically.

If you have ConvertKit, you don't need a separate system for keeping track of your leads and customers, and what relationship they have with you or your business.

These are the features of ConvertKit service that I love the most.

- Send emails that look personal and are easy to read on mobile too.

- Powerful email automation that helps you target specific customers.

- Choose exactly who should receive your broadcast emails through custom segmenting.

- Send emails to everyone who is interested in a particular product, while excluding everyone who has already purchased.

- Beautiful and flexible opt-in forms that automatically change width depending on where you place them.

- Good-looking and easily customizable landing pages.

#8. ClickFunnels

Whatever your business model or niche, you have to have a sales funnel in place - see Chapter 8 on how to build yours.

Trust me, you have one, even if you don't realize it yet. But it's important to review and optimize your sales funnels if you want your online business to grow and have the impact that you want it to have.

ClickFunnels is the tool I turn to for this. The founder believes you don't even need a website to run your business, you can use landing or sales pages, or a Facebook page to collect leads and make sales.

These are some of the features I like most from ClickFunnels.

- It replaces your website, shopping cart, and autoresponder software saving you thousands of dollars.

- Drag and drop page editor that lets you create landing pages and sales pages that look exactly like you want.

- Pick from ready-made sales funnel templates and simply replace with your own content and links.

- Gives you everything you need to market, sell, and deliver your products online.

- Integrates easily with most CRMs, sales cart providers, and autoresponder softwares.

- No more IT support or admin work needed.

ClickFunnels, has the potential to manage every kind of sales funnel you can imagine. From a simple opt-in and thank you page for collecting leads, to a content series based funnel with multiple upsells.

There are pre-designed webinar, product launch and book launch funnels you can just copy and edit, which saves you a ton of time and energy, and negates the need to figure it out on your own, like I had to when I started out.

Also, it offers its own email marketing systems and affiliate management if you chose that tier.

#9. Teachable

I have always been a fan of WordPress, so I've used special plugins to host courses on their own Wordpress sites for over four years.

The problem becomes complicated when you have multiple online courses, as it can cost a lot to setup and customize, and then you need to do continual updates and security maintenance.

Once I got clear on the fact that I will have multiple online courses to cater to the different needs of my audience, I realised I needed to create a seamless experience between all the different courses.

I didn't want to deal with setting up multiple pages, across different systems, dealing with tech support for each of them, and replying to every customer support query because some integration broke.

That is why I ended up choosing Teachable as my preferred choice for a selling and delivering online courses.

Teachable, takes care of everything from the sales page to checkout page, to payment systems, and of course, actually hosting the course content. Also, their user interface (from an end-user point of view) is minimalist, beautiful, and easy to use.

These are some of the additional benefits of selling and delivering your online courses through Teachable.

- Use custom domains to set up your courses, without the teachable branding.

- Highly customizable course sales pages, as well course content pages.

- Easily upload multimedia files directly or import from Dropbox.

- Create quizzes and discussion forums within the course.

- Create your own coupons and promotions.

- Set up course pricing the way you want – one time, monthly, annual, etc.

- Accept international payments and even set up multiple currency support for the same course.

- Comprehensive dashboard with course engagement and student information statistics.

- No need to worry about hosting or security or technical problems.

#10. Zoom

Back in the day I used Skype to conduct podcast interviews, coaching calls and making calls to overseas phones. Then Zoom came along and I was an instant convert.

I use this video conferencing and meeting tool on a daily basis for team meetings, catch-ups with friends and entrepreneurs, hosting live group coaching calls, and recording screen-sharing videos for programs or your team SOPS, as well as interviews for my programs.

Zoom, also has webinar functionality that you can pay extra for. The interface is incredibly clean and sexy and a simple URL link means you can start a meeting anywhere, anytime in both audio, video or both. You can record every meeting with ease too, which is so important for me personally.

Filling In The Gaps

Now that we've gone over some of the top tools, it's time to identify your gaps and selecting tools to streamline your business.

What I constantly see is people joining every social network, downloading and trying out every single new piece of software or application and then, never coming back to use them again.

Instead, they end up with all these login details that they are hopefully saving on Lastpass for tools they don't ever incorporate.

If you take a good hard look at which tools you use on a daily basis, those are pretty much the primary tools that are probably helping you out.

What you need to do is really know your system gaps and then fill them. It's a little bit like looking at a company overview organization chart. When you first start out in business, you are the CEO, you are the assistant, you are the finance person, the marketing person, you are the sales person and slowly as you build your team, you fill those gaps.

The same applies with tools, software and applications helping you with your system.

So start out by looking at the different areas of your business.

- Team management tools

- Finance setup

- Website and operations

- Sales and marketing

If you actually look at your online business and break it down into departments, like an organization, that's how I typically look at my business and then, source and test tools that fit our needs, that have addons and integrate well with other tools we already use - this is key.

Be Disciplined

You need to be disciplined about how you are using all these tools if you want true freedom. I see a lot of people using them in the wrong way.

So here are a few quick tips on how to feel more in control and productive on a daily basis.

#1. Work With The Tools That Fit Your Business Model, Forget The Rest

You'll start to notice a pattern of tools that you are using daily and I'd suggest you write down the ten tools that you are using every single day.

Take a note of those and look at those and where they fit into your business and what is lacking.

#2. Invest Time Learning The Full Features

We've all done it. We've all downloaded a piece of software or started using an application and tried to get to grips with it. But because we never took time to watch videos, watch a tutorial on YouTube or look at their help information we never utilize the tool to the best of its ability.

I mean how often do you actually go through and look at whether you are using Gmail or Asana efficiently? What I would suggest is that once a week, or even once a month, you take one of these tools that you are using and see if there's any updates that allows you to use it in a better way, more optimized way.

In your audit, look closely at how these tool and systems are working for you and ask yourself, "Why am I using this one, it's not really helping me and am not seeing any results if I look at my goals for the year." Or ask,

"Is this helping and streamlining what I'm doing or am I just spending a lot of time on it?"

Or you may realize, "Wow, this is saving me ton of time, my team is using it really well. Are there any associated tools that I can use or any plugins for this tool that comes with it to help me streamline further?"

For example, XERO syncs with many other tools, you are likely already using, to make your accounting even easier. That way everything you are doing and using becomes streamlined and in sync online.

This will make you feel and become more productive and allow you to create some systems in your business that make everything more efficient.

I hope you are now excited to implement some of these smart systems that will make the job of running your business more fun. But before I let you run off all excited to play with these new toys, I want to bring a few things to your attention.

As I mentioned before, there are tools and systems available for every single task in your business. However, that doesn't mean that you need all of them. Investing in systems has to be a business decision, and I'd advise you to keep the following three things in mind.

#1 What's The Return On Investment?

The biggest concern that entrepreneurs have, when investing in tools, is how much it will cost them. That is a valid concern, of course, but more than the cost I would ask you to think of it as return on investment.

If a system can save five hours of your time every week, you can then use those five extra hours to create more content for your online courses.

In one month you can save 20 hours, which is more than enough to create a short video course that you may be able to sell for $50. If you manage to sell the course to even 10 people, that's a total of $500.

That's $500 you wouldn't have been able to make if you had not invested in that particular system. Wouldn't you say it's worth paying $99/month for it?

#2 Does It Make Sense To Pay For The Downtime And Backup Systems?

All these systems may make the job of running your business easier, but it takes time to set them up in the beginning. If you already have a few systems, but are looking to switch over to better ones, the downtime is going to be a concern.

For example, migrating my large list of subscribers from InfusionSoft to ConvertKit, took nearly a month. But I was still paying for InfusionSoft and Mailchimp while it happened because I needed to send emails to my audience and customers.

But since then, I've managed to cancel out and get refunds on a myriad of tools and systems I no longer needed and was still paying for them.

In my case, the technical problems I had when I used to use InfusionSoft cost me thousands of dollars in revenue.

I do not want to be in the same situation when my next launch comes around, so it made sense for me to switch over to the new systems.

Since my business is almost completely online, I can not afford to make this switch without having backups in place. The way I see, it is an investment in the future of my business.

You might want to consider if it makes business sense for you to invest in or upgrade to a new system.

#3 Are The Tools You Are Using Serving Your Needs?

I'll be the first to admit that I was really surprised last month when I saw how much I had paid over the entire year for all the systems and tools I was using. I realised I had been paying for things that I wasn't using anymore, or had bought some new ones that could replace a few older tools.

As you know by now, I am a huge fan of implementing smart systems to streamline my business, so I regularly test out different tools just for the fun of it. But from a purely business perspective, they don't always serve my needs.

For example, I loved LeadPages, but now that I have invested in ClickFunnels and Teachable, I don't need LeadPages anymore.

Your case might be a little different. Let's say you have a service business where you need to have multiple meetings in a week with your clients, with prospects, and with other service providers.

Instead of wasting time emailing back and forth between all of them, you could simply set up a premium account at Calendly.com, which will cut down on all of that and free up more time for the real value generating activity — the actual calls.

Just because a system or a tool, looks cool doesn't mean you have to invest in it. I always recommend trying them out if they offer a free trial. If you find they make your life and business easier, then, by all means, go for it.

What You Learned In This Chapter:

- The benefits of systemizing your business so it can run without you.

- Your Master Operations Manual and why you need it.

- How to quickly create smart Standard Operating Procedures.

- The top 10 tools I use to effectively run my business.

- The best way to choose which tools are right for you.

12

THE KEYS TO LIVING THE FREEDOM LIFESTYLE

Do you know the secret to more freedom in your life?

Discipline.

Ironic, isn't it?

Several years ago, I learned that the more disciplined I was, the more freedom I had.

When I was bouncing around the world, with no set agenda in mind, no routine, schedule or any boundaries to guide me, I actually didn't feel free.

I spent a lot of energy making decisions *every* single day about what to wear, what to pack, what to eat, where to go, how to get there, who to see, what to do, etc.

Now, if you're doing this for a two week holiday, it's incredibly fun because it's outside of your normal routine.

But when traveling is your life, and you do it every day, it can become quite tedious and tiring.

In fact, I know of several long time digital nomads, who've lived on the road, in no fixed abode, for years, even decades, who've recently said, "Enough."

It was fun in the beginning; it gave them incredible experiences, but recently, they just yearned to settle down, have a base, have some familiarity around them, and establish a routine that required less constant effort.

Like Jennifer Lachs, Founder of DigitalNomadGirls.com who had been traveling with her boyfriend for nearly two years as backpackers before they became location independent and started working and traveling as digital nomads.

> "Previously, we'd been jumping from country to country every 2–3 weeks. That's totally fine for backpackers, but once we started working online we realised we'd have to adjust our travel style. So, we decided to slow down a bit and began to stay in most places for about a month.

> But, after 18 months of being on the road and working at that pace, we were simply exhausted. At the same time, I had also started transitioning from freelance work to starting my own business and found it very difficult to build something from scratch while moving around so much."

They decided to it was time to stay put for a while and chose Las Palmas, Spain, as a home base. They originally planned to stay for about 6 months, but ended up staying well over a year, while taking a few month-long trips here and there.

While it's been quite an adjustment, they've loved being able to make close friends and feel like a part of a local community again, go to their favourite restaurants, cafes, and yoga teacher, and establish a routine.

> "One side effect of having a homebase that I hadn't expected was the feeling that I wasn't a 'proper' digital nomad anymore. It sounds crazy, as there's no right or wrong way to be one, but it made me think about how I define this lifestyle for myself. I am learning to listen to myself and trust my gut. When I start getting itchy feet again, that'll means it's time for another adventure.

I think the most important thing is to be flexible and have the freedom to decide. If that means having a home base for a few years, or even long-term, then that's totally fine. If it means traveling faster for a few months or a year, that's also cool. That's the beauty of this lifestyle, we can each define it for ourselves and make changes when we need them."

I so get where Jennifer is at. It took me close to transition to my *new* identity after being the Suitcase Entrepreneur for so long.

In the beginning of 2017, I realised I'd created too much freedom for myself. I was free to do whatever I wanted.

So free, in fact, I couldn't decide what to do after heading off to Bali to run my Freedom Mastermind retreat, and share my birthday with friends and family.

Should I head to Portugal, where I recently bought a house and spend the summer there writing, reading, surfing, and taking a business sabbatical?

Or should I look for a lifestyle property in New Zealand, with my partner and, settle down, grow a garden, learn about permaculture, and finally get a dog and some chickens?

Both versions of my life were distant from each, but equally appealing; it resulted in paralysis. I could not make a decision. I was stuck.

That was quite stressful, until I sat back and realised how ridiculous the whole situation was.

How lucky was I to have this amazing choice in front of me?

Yet, what I actually wanted was fewer options to make it easier to make a decision.

I simply wanted someone to come up to me and say, "Natalie, I think you should stay in New Zealand for the next 12 months and see how that feels."

Even that prompt alone would have set some limitations within, which I could operate with more freedom.

Why? Because I would then have had one location to focus on, and within that location I had less choices, with which, I could make decisions about my lifestyle and business.

Buying our dream property, moving in together and getting dogs and chickens turned my life around 360 degrees. It showed me that you can find freedom in whatever lifestyle you choose.

The Freedom Routine

When you have a purpose, and a vision, and you know where you're going, it becomes much easier to do, without effort.

Easy, as it may sound, I don't always get this right. That's because:

The Real Key To Freedom Is Discipline

Routines, boundaries, and making your own rules, that you have to stick to, helps cut down the number of decisions you have to make, and things you have to think about.

These self imposed limitations will enable you to focus on doing less of the time-wasting, soul-sucking, procrastination-driven activities that are currently filling your days.

It's about doing less. But MORE of the meaningful things.

That's where a powerful daily morning routine is so important. It lets you set the intention for your day ahead.

The right morning routine for you can not only energize you and make you more successful, it can also make you happier and give you true peace of mind.

I'm a firm believer that EVERYONE can be a morning person, even those people who swear they can't function without coffee or a shower first thing.

Why? Because I've seen 'not-a-morning' person get up at 4 am and take action when they have to catch an early morning flight! That's proof that it's a change in mindset, and a change in the stories you tell yourself, and a habit.

My Morning Routine

Over the years I've worked out what works best for me. These days I have my energising morning routine that goes like this...

1. Wake at 5:30am and stretch out in bed like a cat - feels amazing.

2. Drink a large glass of water.

3. Do 20-30 minutes of yoga, weights or stretching.

4. Take a hot shower and finish with a cold burst of water for 30 seconds to wake up my whole body.

5. Make a warm water and lemon drink, and have my daily greens shot.

6. Spend 15 minutes planning my day ahead using our LifePilot.co system.

7. 7:00am - Start on my three most important actions from the Life Pilot daily goals I've set, and using 25 minute Pomodoro sessions to batch the time I work.

8. Regularly stretch or do a short burst of exercise, spontaneous dancing or playing with my dog for 5 minutes after each Pomodoro session.

9. 10am - Have a healthy breakfast or smoothie. (Note: I do intermittent fasting for greater energy and focus).

10. Continue with MIA #2 or #3

I often find, come midday, I've achieved an incredible amount of focused work and momentum. I can choose to do a few hours of project work, creative work, financials, marketing or team related tasks - whatever I set myself for that day.

3-4pm is active time when I exercise, enjoy time with my gorgeous dogs by getting out in nature for a walk or run and recharge my energy levels.

I then do a 20 minute meditation to revitalize my mind!

I can then step back in to do some more work if I wish, or not. But one thing is for sure, 7pm is laptops away and offline time to spend with my loved ones.

It's made a huge difference to our lives - better quality of sleep, more focus, more productive, healthier, happier and joyful.

As part of our Life Pilot process, each Sunday Josh and I look at our weekly goals and reflect on the following prompts or questions

- What were the roses, thorns and bananas (surprises)?

- What was my biggest accomplishment?

- Where did I make the most progress?

- What was the biggest thing I learned?

- What do I want to change for the week ahead

- What are five things I am deeply grateful for?

We've both noticed that reflection and gratitudes are even more effective when you do them daily, along with setting your three most important actions for the day.

You Have Got To Find The Right Morning Routine For YOU

You need to stay true to doing what feels best and making every day one where you feel like a million dollars!

To help you get an idea of what kind of things work for different people, I asked my community of Freedomists about their daily freedom habit or ritual. Here are some of them…

- "I schedule whitespace each month before anything else. More than I think I'll need. It's non-negotiable. This is time when nothing is planned or needs to happen. It's not easy, because I like to plan, achieve and be moving forward, but I've learned that it's what I need to thrive.

- On a daily basis I do art journaling for 15 minutes. This is like a written journal, but instead I paint, collage, doodle or whatever feels right. For me the freedom is in having no fixed outcome in mind just letting go and flow with what happens. A bit like meditation and mindfulness.

- It lets my linear, striving and screen staring brain, take a break. I have a lot going on in my head after working with a client and this allows things to swirl around and make sense in some way. It's re-energising and clears my head. Because I do it every day it's no big deal." ~ *Sarah Kent.*

- "I don't touch my email from Saturday morning to Sunday 8pm, unless I have scheduled in working on the biz project on a Sunday morning. If I do, then I take the equivalent time off during the week. I also don't touch email from 5pm to 8am every weekday. Works a treat" ~ *Fiona Hall.*

- "When I do these 3 things, my focus and productivity go through the roof.

  1. Write out a prioritized to-do list before going to bed. This launches me right into production mode when I sit down to start working in the morning. It also gives my subconscious a head start on the day's projects.

  2. Attack the list, one item at a time. No multitasking.

  3. Create instant momentum by starting with something easy or a project I'm excited about. For me, momentum is everything.

  On the days when I successfully do this, I can get 10 hours of work done in two or three. That leaves most of the day free to do as I please." ~ *Donnie Bryant*

"I very neatly divide my day into creative and business. That's not to say that business isn't creative, it absolutely is, but my business model is basically. 'Make stuff and talk about it,' so the first half of the day is making that stuff, and then the afternoon is about getting it into the world.

I'm up at 5:00 AM every day and stop at 12:00. I break, exercise, nap, shower, etc. Then, 2-5 PM is all business. I take two walks during the day, one at 9:30 AM and another at 4:00 PM.

Anyone on my team can talk to me during these walks, but they absolutely must respect the rules. If it's an AM talk, then business is not allowed. I do not want my brain to be doing any code switching. I want to be firmly in "story mode." Business, brainstorming, admin bullshit, all of that gets handled at the end of the day." ~ *Sean Platt.*

"My thing is walking on the beach at dusk. It's a time to let go, feel the wind and water, be amazed at the beauty of the sunset, watch the little ghost crabs, calm my thoughts and open myself to the opportunities in front of me. This is my personal hour of power." ~ *Brigid Fitzgerald*

"Working in my garden makes me feel free. I like the idea of being able to grow at least some of my own food. It depends on the season and the weather. I do something almost every day, watering, pulling weeds, planting etc. I also like to sit in the garden when the weather is nice and look at the plants or the fabulous view across the valley." ~ *Sif Traustadóttir Rossi*

"I start the day as follows:

1. Drink warm water with lemon.

2. 15-minute meditation.

3. Journaling

4. 30-min walk in the park (often listening to a fab podcast by Natalie).

5. 5-minute quick tidy-up.

6. Update finances.

7. Review goals and MIAs.

Sometimes family or early-morning client commitments, mean I don't do these in exactly this order or immediately one after another, but even when I momentarily go off track,

I can easily go back to where I left off and do these things daily.

It's taken a while to get to this and it's working very well". ~ *Helen Iwata.*

"I use my Daily Focus Card. It's easy to get overwhelmed with all there is to do as a budding entrepreneur. One practical tool that has increased my daily focus, is to use a daily focus card. It's just a 3x5 card that I fill out every morning.

Side 1: My 3 Big Wins - I draw three big boxes and write down the 3 things that would make today a success. I then race to get those three things done before lunch.

Side 2: Daily Schedule & Misc. To Dos - I then draw a line down the middle of the card. On the right side, I write down my schedule for the day from 9 to 5. On the left side, I leave open to writing down any new to-dos that surface during the day, especially while I'm trying to stay focused on my three big wins." ~ *Jonathan Milligan*

As you can see, everyone has their own unique daily routine that allows them to set their intentions for the day, go out and accomplish their daily goals, and enjoy the freedom lifestyle they want.

The common denominator among almost all of them, is starting out with YOU time, followed by focused and condensed work time to achieve more in less time.

I suggest you re-read these routines and create your own unique version, or use lifepilot.co to help you win the day.

If your current daily routine is still not letting you experience the freedom you want, you might actually need a decent break.

If you'd like to take time to pause and reflect on the lifestyle you truly want to create, consider taking a digital sabbatical.

The Power Of A Digital Sabbatical

I've taken a digital sabbatical every year for the last four years, ranging from five days to three months.

It started in Malaysia on Penang Island in 2013, when I thought to myself, what would it be like to take time offline and disconnect completely?

The experience was so incredible I wrote an entire blog post about it. Here's a short excerpt.

> "In the past seven days of my digital sabbatical, I have read nine books, listened to 11 audio interviews, completed my first ever painted picture, mapped out my personal goals, made copious notes about business strategy and launch tactics.
>
> Sweet. I've been more productive, yet also, had more free time than ever.
>
> I slept a lot, including two stints of sleeping 12 hours plus. I've relaxed on the beach, meditated daily, walked in the jungle, swum in the sea, enjoyed a rainforest canopy swing bridge walk, mingled with monkeys and practiced yoga.
>
> I've done a lot of gazing off into the distance, observing and just listening to the sounds of nature. I've eaten fresh fruit, dined three times a day in cafes and restaurants, had a massage, manicure, pedicure and herbal treatment plus had my feet kissed by fish – I kid you not.

It's called a digital sabbatical my friend, and below I'm going to reveal the diaries of my digital sabbatical and how you can apply this too."

Just reading that makes me want to dive into another one today, and I hope it prompts you to consider taking one too, if not more.

Rules Of A Digital Sabbatical

Before you go into your utterly blissful and transformative experience, you do need to set some rules of what's acceptable on your digital sabbatical.

These are unique to you. Only you know your achilles heel when it comes to distractions, being online and temptations.

For someone like me, whose entire business is online, I thought I needed to go a little easy on myself, because anyone who's met me knows I live online.

The great news is, I found it surprisingly easy to disconnect, once I committed to it fully.

Nat's Rules

Not allowed: No email or social media, and no laptop time at all.

Allowed: Downloading new podcast episodes to my smartphone and reading kindle books on my smartphone and iPad.

I can already see your head shaking, and these words coming from your mouth…

You: "Natalie girl, not all of us can just take seven days off, you know!"

Me: "Bollocks, and yes you can. In fact, you probably need to. Your life and business may even depend on it. If you were really strategic, you would have planned several of these sabbaticals to happen this year already. So go do it!"

Productivity is about laser like focus on the things that count.

If you can't take seven days, start with two – your weekend. Yes, it's YOUR weekend, so use it to disconnect.

For my first digital sabbatical, when I finally checked in online, I found less emails than I thought, none of them urgent – read that NONE.

Instead, I found SaneBox, which essentially brings sanity back to your inbox by filtering the unimportant emails. And it only delivers the most important to your inbox (learn more in Chapter 11), had sorted out the crap so I could just focus on replying to the emails that mattered.

My virtual team had held down the fort, my assistant at the time Margaret, had been busy organizing and scheduling coaching sessions with the $100 Change Scholarship winners for me during January, answering queries and taking care of any inquiries.

My Chief Happiness Officer Cher, had been reviewing my content and blog posts and learning more about what makes my business and customers tick. She turned in a report of what she'd done and next steps to take. It was fantastic.

Over on Facebook, friends had gotten married, engaged, fired, hired, gained major media attention, had to deal with a sick kid or just come back from holiday.

Same on Twitter and Google Plus, and thanks to Mailchimp and e-Junkie, people had been able to buy my books and programs without my help. These days I use ConvertKit and Teachable, but whatever works for you.

All was well and once more, I was ready to dive back in with energy and a new found perspective to what was becoming somewhat tiring and overrated before my digital sabbatical.

Disconnecting, priotizing sleep, relaxation, creative time and reflection allows you to reinvigorate, rejuvenate and recharge your mind, body and soul.

Five Steps To Maximize Your Time Off

1. Plan Ahead

Longer periods of disconnect are such a must in this uber-connected world we live in. Real estate mogul Barbara Corcoran, who sold her company for $66 million and invests in others via Shark Tank, takes vacations for one week every four weeks. She swears by them as she gets her best ideas on vacation. Her advice, "Make sure you mark it out in your calendar before the next year." She vacations every four weeks and comes back a better leader, marketer and investor.

2. Make It A Habit

You can reclaim time every day if you simply schedule it in. For example having a 20 minute power nap each afternoon or doing a focused meditation, will ensure you gain greater clarity, creativity and energy.

The thing is you need to view it as an integral part of your week and factor it into your schedule.

Disconnect twice a day or more, like when you go outside for a walk don't take your smartphone and instead just go and play – throw a Frisbee outside, dance around your living room or just do spontaneous handstands or cartwheels like I do.

It's something we suck at doing these days, yet, it's where our creative genius is unleashed. Kids have the wildest imaginations remember, and they play often.

3. Become A Pro

The ah-ha moment I had, while reading Stephen Pressfield's book *Turning Pro*, was that if you're truly committing to changing the world, doing your best work and creating your best art, you need to set up the framework in which to do this every day.

This starts with the discipline to give time to yourself, to focus on your priorities. He talks of the time he took off for a year, with his savings, to write his book. He rented out a place for a year and took to using his typewriter everyday. Did he publish? No.

He wrote page after page for a whole year and ditched the whole lot. But he says that it's the year he turned Pro because he had created the space and discipline, in which to become a better writer and commit to daily practice.

4. Create Boundaries

If there's one thing I realised while disconnecting, it was that once I had all this time on my hands I felt ridiculously free.

Even when you're not disconnecting you can do one incredible thing that will transform your life.

As long as you are purposeful in taking dedicated, meaningful time off from your business, then you are on the right track

If you don't want to work on the weekends, then set that up as your rule, let your clients, friends and family know that you simply won't get back to them until Monday.

Do you want to work half days? Great, then clearly state that in your terms and conditions, on your website, in the footer of your email.

Teach your clients and customers when you're in business mode and when you're in lifestyle mode. They will respect you more for it - trust me.

As Michael Zipursky, CEO of ConsultingSuccess.com told me:

> "One of the hardest, yet best decisions I constantly make is to say, 'No' to a lot of things. When I see the latest technology. Some new course. Someone wanting to promote something together, a new tool, the list goes on...I say 'No.' If it doesn't directly align with the plan we are working on then I pass. While it can take a lot of restraint, it's had a very significant positive impact on our business over the years.
>
> It's allowed us to run a streamlined business, serve clients all over the world, while traveling and working. When I say, 'No' there are a lot less moving parts to the business and we can really focus in and master the most important ones."

Time is one of the most precious commodities we have, and we all get the exact same amount. How you spend your time is up to you.

5. Trust In Your Systems

Let your team take over, and if it's just you right now, then schedule out your social media updates using Buffer or Hootsuite. You put on an autoresponder email so people know you're away, and you field any 'urgent' queries to your trusted team member(s). If you know what your priorities are for the year, you'll also find that most stuff you do is completely unrelated to achieving your goals.

Co-living The Freedom Lifestyle With Friends And Family

If you're choosing the unconventional route of designing your own lifestyle business, you're going to need to understand that many of your friends and family simply won't understand what the heck you're doing.

The thing is, it's really important to understand this before you embark on creating your own Freedom Plan, because it's not often discussed, yet, it may really affects you.

Here's What Happens:

You start out building this business you love, and doing everything to make it work. Meanwhile, you're also spending more time enjoying yourself, perhaps traveling or generally looking like you have a lot more free time on your hands.

To the 'outside' world it looks like you're just having a blast and not working at all. Your family will question if you're throwing your education away or a career path in corporate they'd hope you'd take.

Your friends will question if you are, in fact, working at all and tell you to pull your head in and grow up, or ask you how they can get in on whatever it is you're doing.

That latter group is the one you get to inspire, educate and support if they're willing to take the leap.

That former group….to be straight up with you, they're the ones you're going to have to let go of – unless, they come around and support you no matter what.

The thing is, 90% of people will simply not understand your way of life, or your desire to put freedom first. That's because they're stuck in what I call the 'Muggle' world.

Their world and conventional view of it is what they've been brought up to believe all their life and it looks like this.

- Go to school

- Go to college

- Get into a University

- Get a job

- Buy a car

- Meet a partner

- Get engaged

- Get married

- Buy a house and get a mortgage

- Have kids

- Work hard for the next 40 or so years, to afford the things you need to fill the house you bought and pay off the bills for all the other things you think you need.

- Take 2-3 week vacations each year.

- Mainly work until you retire, to then enjoy the fruits of your labour.

Because that's their world, they will not want you to rock the boat by showing them a better one.

Instead, they will do all in their power to make you feel like you're the one in the wrong, like you're going to fail, like you're being stupid, naive or downright outrageous wanting to pursue the unconventional path to freedom.

That's why you need to take a good, hard look at which friends you truly adore and spend more time with the ones who make your life more abundant, happy and wonderful.

You also need to drop the ones who suck your energy, put you down, criticize your dreams and actions and no longer serve you or understand you.

It sounds harsh, but it's absolutely necessary if you want to be free. Plus, you'll make way for the new people flooding into your life, who totally GET you and what you're doing.

Not only that, but they make you think bigger and see even more opportunities on how to earn money doing what you love, while leading your best lifestyle.

I am frankly stunned that the majority of the Western World still thinks this is the way to live a truly fulfilling life. But if I'm honest with myself, they don't think that at all. It's just that it's all they know.

It's what has been shown to them from their parents, their grandparents, their friends and drummed into them on TV, movies, books and literature from the minute they left the womb.

After a decade of attempting to convince people like these to see what's possible for them, how they can shape and craft their life into something beautiful and that they have the tools they need to do this today, not tomorrow, I've learned one very important thing:

Only YOU can free yourself from the shackles of the traditional world you currently live in and choose the path you want to take.

Once you're ready to evolve, to change, to take control of your life, THEN I can help.

I'm no personal development guru, but I'd like to think I do a pretty decent job of helping people to leave the dark side and 'join the force.'

I have realised two important things:

1. Giving unsolicited advice to people who don't want to hear it, or aren't ready for change is pointless.

2. You will likely outgrow your friends if you choose an unconventional life, but if your friendship is rooted in meaning and common values, you will always enjoy spending time together.

What I do know to be true is that you are going to be far better off spending your time with quality people who get you, who can energize and challenge you, and who are on the same journey as you are.

What You Learned In This Chapter:

- The benefits of morning freedom routine and how to create yours.

- The power of a digital sabbatical to reinvigorate you and your business

- How to surround yourself with 'Freedomists' who support your lifestyle.

CONCLUSION

PUTTING IT ALL TOGETHER INTO YOUR OWN UNIQUE FREEDOM PLAN

Staying true to your chosen lifestyle is probably going to be the number one challenge you face on your Freedom Plan journey.

That's why I urge you to re-read the entire first stage of this book and get really clear on your vision for why you do what you do.

Keep that strong vision front and centre of all you do, so that you set a daily intention for living your ideal lifestyle and having a business or career that supports it.

Surround yourself with people who understand and fully support your unique desire to have your own lifestyle business, to have more time and freedom to be at home with your family, to work unconventional hours, to own less stuff - whatever it is that is important to you.

This is your unique Freedom Plan that you've designed. Now you need to own it.

Whenever you're feeling lost or less free than you'd like, I suggest you view this as a three-stage approach to getting back on track - as this book has been designed to help you do.

Stage 1: Freedom Mindset

Tap into the power of daily meditation and visualization of your perfect day and I promise you you'll see real changes and shifts happening.

Combine this with being very clear on your values and what's most important to you. This will ensure you stay on your own path to achieving your Freedom Plan.

Revisit the first four chapters of this book to help you strengthen your belief in yourself and tap into your unique superpower. That way you'll stay in flow more often when you're dealing with your work, your team and even your loved ones.

Stage 2: Freedom Business

Your business will be guided by your transforming mindset. As you become more clear on your true desires and guided by your new mindset and beliefs, your business will naturally shift with you.

Armed with your new found knowledge about the best way to structure your business and monetise your natural talents, you will make better choices about your revenue streams and areas, in which, you are spending your time.

Delegation will come more freely to you and with it, a greater trust in the right people you'll hire and the systems you've put in place.

Personally, you'll find a new level of productivity and structure that leads to more time off, a greater sense of achievement and a better balance in your everyday world between work and play.

Stage 3: Freedom Lifestyle

All of the above, will lead to a level of discipline that gives you the freedom you desire.

With your systems and team in place, your objective will be aimed at continuing to scale your business, while consciously removing yourself from it, and spending time doing more of the things you love.

Your daily freedom routine you've created, will continue to pay you dividends as your Freedom Plan evolves with you.

So what next?

Choose Your Winning Freedom Mindset. It Is As Simple As That.

Simply choose to live your best possible life. Do not settle for mediocrity any longer. You have just one life.

Stop making excuses. There's no room for them on your Freedom Plan.

Start taking action and continue to define what your ideal lifestyle looks like.

Focus on how good you feel when you accept the fact that life is completely in your control and accept all the power you have within you to accomplish great things.

Come Join Me!

If you've made it this far. Congratulations, you're well on your way to becoming a Freedomist. What can do you to continue the momentum?

1. **Join the free Freedom Plan companion video series** that's designed especially to dig deeper into what I've covered in this book at thefreedomplan.co/start

2. **Access the full list of resources included in this book** on the next pages, and head to thefreedomplan.co/resources anytime to access them too. My team and I will do our very best to continually update them.

Say Hello And Let's Connect Here:

twitter.com/nataliesisson

instagram.com/nataliesisson

facebook.com/groups/freedomistcollective

nataliesisson.com

It's been an honour to lead you on this adventure and I look forward to hearing all about your own unique Freedom Plan when we meet in person, somewhere around the world.

Natalie xo

ACKNOWLEDGEMENTS

This book has been a long time in the making. It all started out back in July 2014 when I ran the first pilot of the Freedom Plan program. After teaching hundreds of students over the next three years, the idea for this book came to life.

I dedicate this book to the hundreds of amazing Freedom Plan alumni members whose challenges, wins and results were inspiring and shaped my understanding, learning, teaching and coaching of this framework.

Special thanks go to the initial copy edits of the draft manuscript by Debashish Das, Linda Gilbert, Leann McKeown, Rivka Kawano, Martin Hughes and Michelle Frost.

Huge thanks and respect go to Ian Borges who made a number of great recommendations to the final manuscript I included and Pepper Gross for her attention to detail.

To Guy Vincent and Lee Constantine at Publishizer, your ongoing support and commitment to this book after my successful crowdfunding campaign, and to finding me the right publisher, was nothing short of amazing.

To the wonderful humans who pledged to that campaign and in doing so told me this book mattered and need to be out in the world, then patiently waited for the damn thing to come out, you have my eternal gratitude.

These are:

Aamer Iqbal, Caroline Ceniza-Levine, Zena Bruges, Amanda Workman, Dai Manuel, Dan Norris, Catherine Newton, Chris Guillebeau, Helen Iwata, Karen Wojciechowski, Cathy Goddard, Karen Gunton, Dave Greenberg, Osmaan Sharif and Hayden Glass.

Jeff Ghaemaghamy, Foundr Magazine, Saeema Salim, Jenny Plant, Elisa Doucette, Debi Auger, Amy Mitchell, Désirée Fawn, Gudrun Lauret, Jan Moore, Diana Tedoldi, Elisa Khoo, Dov Gordon, Karen Hardie, Seema Bharwani, Donna Partow, Kirsten Thompson, Seth Kaplowitz, Patricia Erlandson, Steve Chou, Toby Jenkins and Laura Trotta.

Drew Westcott, Erin Davy, Oddgeir Engdal, Holly Worton, Davina Gilbert, Gwen Elliot, Harry Hansen, Amanda Craig, Bruna Baptista, Pamela L'heureux, Chris Hurwitz, Debbie Wood, Gregory Brown, Agnieszka Parr, John Young, Amanda Geary, Janina Jaworek, Amber Baines, Tom Andrews, Gudrun Lauret, Jason VanOrden, Sergio Sala, Erin Davy, David Rigby, Charles Murray, Gareth Foster, Robert Mares, Joe Taylor, Karen Creighton, Lyndal Meehan, Maria Nicholas, Lauren Parsons, Jeremy Parkin, Kirsty Bartholomew, Laura Jasmin, Matt Jones and Kate Peterson.

Jon Watkins, Caroline Chasle Brook, Alicia Michelle, Anfernee Chansamooth, Dan Flower, Jonathan Roberts, Amanda Ewin, Frederick Liew, Emma Cox, Christine Oser, Girish Kumar, Claire Rouger & Rosemary Kimani, Shane Croteau, Andrew Easter, Laura Dick, Erin Gall, Daniel Krebs, Sebastien Langelier, Christopher Peden, Tanya McGillFreeman, Andy Willis, June Molina, Helen Rebello, Tim Wolf, Sylwia Sek, Jane Leggate, Kate Williams, Angela Clancy, Jesse Krieger, David Cole, Greg Hoppe, Mary Goldsmith, Navid Moazzez, Laurens Bonnema, Marjorie Crawford and Lori Ann DeLappe-Grondin.

Gretchen Howell, Shawn Smith, Imke van Kuppeveld, Jake Woehlke, Aniruddha Railkar, Jessica Swann, Bryan, Carina Allen, Jodie Hurst, Kat Jenkins, John Rogers, Carmel Mckenzie, David Allan, Toni Jessop, Frank

Peter, Glen Thomson, James Frank, Katie Brockhurst, Anitra Powell, Mike Strock, Sue Parker, Grant Miller, Yvonne Turner, Christopher Bergeron, Kate Savory, Daniella, Aubrey Perez, Stacey Gavin, Yael Fingal, Ian Webber, Joanne Amos, Brian Baulch, Rhys Hearne, Corena Bahr, Nadine Nelen, Katrina Redford, Jill Kraft, Dana Rederis, Gordon Philips, Rodrigo Perez and Scott Burgess.

Sheryn Murray, Carol Metanczuk, Tommy Crowley, Joni Rose, Clare Wilson, Mark Mercer, Kevin Hassett, Jordan Gibbings, Igor Yovenko, John Lee, Liz Dare, Mandi Ellefson, Jackie Smith, Marilyn Miranda, Roel Arnold, Clare Harrison, Nathalie Lussier, Julie Nabaala, Kimberly Roulo, Lauren Dulin, Jacqui Coward, Kath Crow, Michelle Bailey, Pete McKillop, Theo Olifiers, Jan Demsar, Sharon Smith, PL Woodward, MTS Zuydgeest, Russell James, Saira Jamal, Sarah Allsopp, Laurna Munro, Martin Hughes, Rob Bazinet, Sam Jiwani, Micah Rich, Jane White, Nancy Scuri, LeeAnna Adkins and Mike Goncalves.

Nicola Brown, Sarah Allsopp, Prarinya K, Stephanie Hautcoeur, Leah Bateman, Nicola Moss, Robert Simplicio, Tammi Gaw, Linda Trapasso, Stacey Chapman, Mikki Wiley, Tia Lloyd, Nick Bradfield, Rob Kornblum, Simon Reimler, Robin Lehman, Tamera DeCenso, Sisse Skytte, Mark Stamas, Sarah Zee, Travis Belton, Sasha Peakall, Nicole Joseph, Lisa Bloom, Mary Mumm, Rudy Rumohr, Tanja Fritzensmeier, Victoria Toogood, Mike Goncalves, Lisa Fuqua, Mary Czarnecki, Nikola Case, Patti Nelson, Mike Mahlan and Stephen Back.

Richard Szarvas, Paul Byrne, Tara Jackson, Leanne Moon, Tara Ciecko, Mark Major, Lee Nazal, Nikki Love, Robin Harp, Mikki Wiley, Leigh Twine, Martina Barusic, Moriamo Onabanjo, Nicola Rankin, Vernon Delpesce, Wayne Panniello, Xieurx Concepcion, Lisa O'Connell, Marvin Abisia, Paul Einarsen, MindXventures, Rob Williger, Nicole Wijngaarden, Ronsley Vaz, Samantha Thomas and Melinda Hammond.

To every person who generously opened up to provide a case study or offered up a piece of wisdom in this book and allowed me to shine the light on them to be a beacon for others creating their own Freedom Plan - I salute you.

These wonderful humans include:

Nicola Rankin, David Harder, Rob Garrett, Sif Traustadóttir, Mirian Bocija Sanchez, Sasha Peakall, Derek Murphy, Audie Cashion, Justin Krane and Nora Dunn.

Erin McNeaney, Paul & Sheryl Shard, Jo Bendle, Jasper Ribbers, Greg and Rachel Denning, Richard Patey, Felix Page, Natalie Cutler-Welsh, Dr. Alexis Shields, Sylvia van de Logt, Dov Gordon, Michael Zipursky, Jonathan Milligan, Matt McWilliams, Gene Hammett, Tera Maxwell, Adam Franklin, Toby Jenkins, Donnie Bryant, David Finkel, Laura Roeder, Mandi Ellefson, Jennifer Lachs, Sarah Kent, Fiona Hall, Sean Platt, Brigid Fitzgerald and Joseph Bushnell.

Thanks to Justin Sachs, founder of Motivational Press, for seeing the potential in this book and working with me to birth it to the world.

To my family for always being there for me. What would I do without your love, hugs, laughter and guidance. You've seen me create my own Freedom Plan, from quitting my job to building my business, to my next life stage and you supported me no matter what I chose to do. For that unwavering freedom, I love you most.

Finally to my love, Joshua Vial, for showing me a new way of thinking, acting and understanding. Your intellect, deep love and eternal calm has been the perfect tonic for my never-ending action-taking and energy.

Your total belief in all I do and all I'm yet to do makes me stronger, wiser and my most expansive self. I can't wait to see what else we discover together.

RESOURCES

You can use this mini summary section, to refer back to as a quick reference tool for any resource I've mentioned throughout the book such as, checklists, downloads, books, websites, apps, tools and services.

To make it even easier, head to thefreedomplan.co/resources to find the most up to date list of everything in this book 24/7.

To dive deeper into what you've learned, and to bring this book to live, make sure you sign up for my free companion video series at thefreeddomplan.co/start.

Chapter 1. The Freedom Mindset And How To Make Your Dream Life A Reality

The Surprising Truth About Freedom

State of the Global Workplace study

Nat and Jodie, House Sitting Academy

Chapter 3: Creating And Designing Your Perfect Day

Yoga with Adriene

DownDog

Daily Yoga

———

Yogaglo

Nicola Rankin, Habit Sculptor

David Harder, Pleasure Center

Rob Garrett, Robofficeninja.com

Sif Traustadóttir, Sifthevet.com

Mirian Bocija Sanchez, Mirianbsanchez.com

Book:

The Code of the Extraordinary Mind by Vishen Lakhiani

Chapter 4: Using Your Unique Superpowers To Design Your Freedom Business

Osmaan Sharif, Rapidtransformation.co.uk

Wealth Dynamics Profile test

Gretchen Rubin, gretchenrubin.com

Gretchen Rubin's Quiz: The Four Tendencies

Don Clifton, CliftonStrengths 34 Test

Sally Hogshead, Fascination Advantage assessment

Jo Bendle, jobendle.com

Books:

Awaken the Giant Within by Tony Robbins

Think and Grow Rich by Napoleon Hill

The Four Tendencies: The Indispensable Personality Profiles That Reveal How to Make Your Life Better (and Other People's Lives Better, Too) by Gretchen Rubin

StrengthsFinder 2.0 by Tom Rath

How the World Sees You: Discover Your Highest Value Through the Science of Fascination by Sally Hogshead

Chapter 5: Monetizing You And Building Your Expert Platform

FundRazr

Camtasia

Optimize Press

Book:

The Suitcase Entrepreneur Book

Chapter 6. Choosing The Right Revenue Streams For Financial Freedom

Airbnb

Book Yourself Solid by Michael Port

Everbooked

Beyond Pricing

Payfully

Shopify

WP Curve

ConvertKit

ClickFunnels

Teachable

Trail Wallet

Poochable.com

Amazon FBA

TradeMe

Books:

Get Paid for Your Pad by Jasper Ribbers

Coffee Shop Entrepreneurs by Richard Patey

Book Yourself Solid by Michael Port

Sail Away! A Guide to Outfitting and Provisioning for Cruising

Nora Dunn, The Professional Hobo

Erin McNeaney, Never Ending Voyage

Paul & Sheryl Shard, Distant Shores Television

Greg and Rachel Denning, Worldschool Family

Richard Patey, Bootstrapping Online Business

Natalie Cutler-Welsh, Go to Girl Ltd

Sylvia van de Logt, 40PlusStyle.com

Felix Page, Clicks Academy

Chapter 7: Your One-Page "Miracle" Business Plan That Really Works

WPEngine

Hostgator

XERO

PayPal

Stripe

One Page Miracle Business Plan

Google Analytics

Audie Cashion, World Peace Center

Justin Krane, A money strategist for business owners

Chapter 8: Building A Lucrative Sales Funnel And Automating Your Business.

'Are you cut out to be a freedom entrepreneur' quiz

KingSumo

Dropbox

Sasha Peakall, The Sales Funnel Strategist

Derek Murphy, CreativIndie

Russell Brunson, russellbrunson.com

Chapter 9: How To Scale Your Business Without You

David Finkel

Toggl

Canva

Slack

Google Apps

Zapier

Right2Freedom.com

Matt McWilliams, mattmcwilliams.com

Dr. Alexis Shields, dralexisshields.com

Books:

Scale: Seven Proven Principles to Grow Your Business and Get Your Life Back by Jeff Hoffman

Who by Geoffrey Smart

Chapter 10: Finding, Hiring And Building Your Global Dream Team

Slack

Google Apps

Zapier

Right2Freedom.com

Matt McWilliams, mattmcwilliams.com

Dr. Alexis Shields, dralexisshields.com

Who by Geoffrey Smart

Tailwind

Upwork

Remote

Fiverr

Asana

Trello

What's App

Telegram

Google Suite

One Drive

Coschedule

Toby Jenkins, Bluewire Media

Chapter 11: Smart Systems To Streamline Your Time And Make You More Effective

Wordpress

ConvertKit

Mailchimp

Calendly

Loom

The Ultimate Guide on how to use Asana to become a productivity and task management genius

Lastpass

Asana

Sanebox

Zoom

Leadpages

Trello

Book:

Work the System by Sam Carpenter

Chapter 12: Your Daily Freedom Routine

Jennifer Lachs, DigitalNomadGirls.com

Sarah Kent, Sarah-Kent.com

Fiona Hall, Kiffin

Donnie Bryant, Co-founder of Email Copy Boss

Sean Platt, Sterling & Stone

Brigid Fitzgerald, BeInspiredLiving.com

Helen Iwata, SasugaCommunications.com

Sif Traustadóttir Rossi, sifthevet.com

Jonathan Milligan, Blogging Your Passion

Barbara Corcoran, BarbaraCorcoran.com

Michael Zipursky, CEO of Coach to Elite Consultants

Lifepilot.co

Hootsuite

Book:

Turning Pro by Steven Pressfield

ABOUT THE AUTHOR

Natalie Sisson is a Freedomist, entrepreneur, bestselling author, sought-after speaker, and one of 50 Must-Follow Women entrepreneurs in 2017, according to Huffington Post.

After eight years in the corporate world, Natalie Sisson left her high paying job in business development to join the entrepreneurial world as a cofounder of a technology startup in Canada.

Desiring even more, she went on to start her blog and business, The Suitcase Entrepreneur, in April 2010. In a few short years she turned it into a thriving multiple six-figure education lifestyle business she could run from just a laptop and her smartphone, from anywhere in the world.

Driven by her desire to obtain what most value so highly, but few achieve – ultimate – freedom, she spent the first two years hustling like crazy, making the same mistakes most new business owners do and learning a lot of hard lessons before she developed the blueprint to building a thriving online business and lifestyle.

Now, Natalie teaches thousands of entrepreneurs around the world to fast track their own business success and design a lifestyle they love through content, books, courses, group coaching and speaking.

Natalie is a contributor to Thrive, Forbes and Lifehack and has been featured on many other publications and media outlets including 60 Minutes, Yahoo Finance, Huffington Post, Guardian, Daily Mail, Sydney Herald, Mashable and more.

Originally from Wellington, New Zealand, Natalie has citizenship in the United Kingdom and has travelled to 70 countries to date and lived on 5 continents, all while running her business and living out of a suitcase.

Since April 2017 she lives on a beautiful property in New Zealand with her entrepreneurial partner Josh. Together they enjoy their 2.5 acres of land and garden, two gorgeous white German Shepherds and chickens.

She considers Portugal her second home now and owns a house there and regularly visits to enjoy the relaxed lifestyle and surfing.

Her favourite claims to fame, are winning a Regional Body Sculpting competition in 2004, a Gold Medal in Beach Ultimate Frisbee in 2007, breaking a World Record in Dragon Boating in 2007. And of course starting her first business in 2010, with nothing, but a hope, a dream and a desire to create her own Freedom Plan.

CPSIA information can be obtained
at www.ICGtesting.com
Printed in the USA
BVHW051404091118
532163BV00010B/139/P